DATE

MAR 2 7 1985

THE CONFESSION WRITER'S HANDBOOK

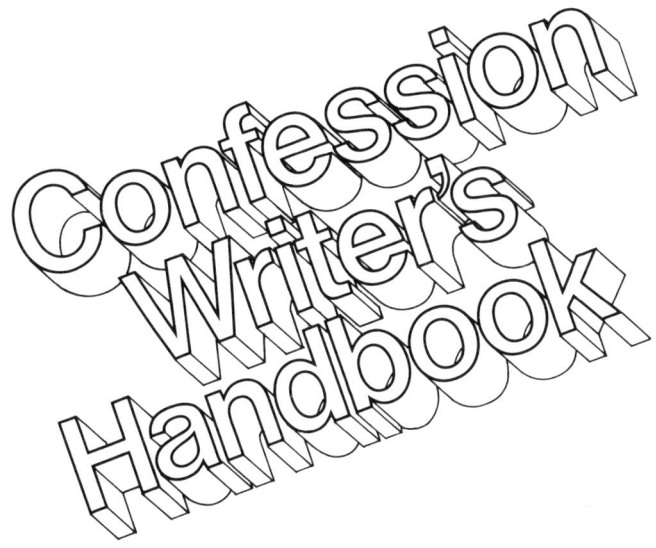

by
Florence K. Palmer

Writer's Digest, 9933 Alliance Drive, Cincinnati, Ohio 45242

Library of Congress Cataloging in Publication Data
Palmer, Florence K.
  The confession writer's handbook.
  1. Confession stories — Authorship. I. Title.
  PN3377.5.C6P3   808'.025   75-30884
  ISBN 0-911654-29-1

International Standard Book No. 0-911654-29-1
Published by
Writer's Digest, 9933 Alliance Rd., Cincinnati OH 45242
Copyright© 1975 by Florence K. Palmer
Printed and bound in the United States of America

All rights reserved. No part of this book may be reproduced in any manner whatsoever without written permission from the publisher, except by reviewers who may quote brief passages to be printed in a magazine or newspaper.

*For confession writers everywhere —
may our tribe increase.*

Acknowledgments

Special thanks to Lynne Ellinwood, who shared a conference panel, and saw a possible book in my approach to the Confession; to Richard Rosenthal, my publisher, who is a joy to work with; to Henry Malmgreen, editor and friend, who "midwifed" this handbook; and to Florence J. Moriarty, who encouraged a very new confessioneer, and has proved to me in the years since that confession editors really are the friendliest.

Space limits individual mention of all the friends, writers and editors who have also contributed so much in so many ways to the experience in these pages, but particular acknowledgment is made to my long-time writing friends, Ruth MacLeod, Louise Boggess, and Grace Hendron, who are always there when I need advice or assistance; to the late Edith Margolis, my agent, who bore with me for nearly twenty-five years; and to my students at Clackamas Community College, who uncomplainingly let themselves be used as a testing-board for *The Confession Writer's Handbook* while it was being written.

PHOTO CREDIT to Betty Philpott.

Foreword

After eighteen years of grinding out 216 issues of Modern Romances, and putting together some 40 odd newsletters designed to enlighten would-be confessions writers, I have a confession of my own to make. I never did quite believe that just anyone could be taught to write good confessions. Writers are born that way, I suspected — not created by the most knowing of teachers. Slush piles, rejects — just the sheer volume of words that pour over any editor's desk in a given year's time induce a measure of skepticism.

For eighteen years I wasn't being paid by my publisher, of course, to teach. I picked and chose, winnowed and gleaned. And every confessions story weakness or shortcoming was tattoed indelibly on my mind. Like a Pavlovian canine, I reacted negatively to hateful narrators, stilted dialogue, cardboard cut-out characters, plots with tired blood, addled motivations.

Everyone and his brother, I thought in my glummer moments, wants to be a confessions writer. But few, responding to this perverse inner call, would be chosen. A lot of sows' ears, I was convinced, and lamentably few silk purses.

This attitude of mine has been rudely shattered by a lady with whom I've corresponded at length — and never met.

Florence K. Palmer, author of this book I hope you'll read, re-read, and take to heart, has written and *sold* confessions for twenty years. But how many selling writers, I ask myself enviously, write like a good teacher and think like a good editor? If confessions writing *can* be taught, Mrs. Palmer has miraculously done it. She makes it tempting, rewarding, and feasible. Be prepared, she warns, to work hard. Amen. Don't concentrate solely, she urges, on cash emoluments. Publishers' checks are necessary proof that you're doing something right. But confess writing, says Mrs. Palmer, is an achievement, a living experience shared with hundreds of thousands of readers. It's a fascinating study course in human behavior with grades based on how much you like people in general and how you relate to them. Amen again. Love not only thy neighbor, but everyone you meet. Empathize, have compassion for all the problems that are part of the human condition.

Listen, feel and record, Mrs. Palmer urges, and you'll be able to create living, storied prototypes whose lives and sorrows and joys readers will want to share.

This is the part of her message, even more than her admirable mastery of confession techniques, that changed me from skeptic to believer. Try hard enough, be guided by her precepts, I'm now the first to concede, and there is no good reason why *you* can't be a successful confessions writer.

—Henry Malmgreen

Contents

Foreword
What got me started writing confessions. The plus values this field offers serious writers. How to use my experiences for your own "confessing."

1 *In the Beginning*   *1*
Three factors — hybrid origin, anonymity and writer's attitude — influence the Confession. Scotch thrift or editorial vision? From Sex to Social Significance — the fifty years between. The New Confession, it's come a long way.

2 *The What and the Who*   7
Major confession categories. Why a confessional format? Keyword and the Aim. Relating the motivating *cause* to the *effect,* or problem. A printer's ink counterpart of the Peace Corps Volunteer in action. What makes the confession writer different? The necessary "TIONS." Adjusting the fit-all short story pattern to the Confession. The "golden thread" of *reader identification* to preserve *confession tone.*

3 *Problem and Theme*   14
Confessions all *problem* stories, the resolution of each its *theme* to give readers new insight into own

flawed life pattern. No original problem, only fresh approach and different focus. Emotional potential essential. Theme implicit in story, grows out of action and dialogue. Sources of themes. The need for "living" people to meet chosen confession problem head-on.

4 *Characterization* 18
Strongest plot contrived-seeming unless characterization is solid. You and your narrator inseparable; your innermost thoughts, emotions and memories give life to hers. Profiles of each key character an aid to "inside-out" writing. Characterization the foundation of all emotional response: *caring* the one emotion toward which every other is built. Characterizing those who influence viewpoint character's actions gives depth to narrator as an individual. Characterization continuous, and much of it written between the lines. Use of *symbols*. "Narrators the Confession Editor doesn't want to meet." *Little things used purposefully,* and looking at the world through narrator's eyes.

5 *Plot* 30
Plot vs. Characterization — neither can function alone. The "I can't plot" bugaboo. Plotting merely *organized conflict,* a road map to get narrator from here to there. *Who, Why, How* and *What* method of formulating story line. Answers to the four plotmaker questions form rough synopsis. Excerpt from a synopsis "fleshed out" to full scene — example.

6 *Opening and Ending* 35
Writer's biggest challenge. 4 W's to *prepare* the reader. Open with action or narration? Where to open in relation to story problem. Know where you're going before you start. Examples of various opening types and formats. The *Ending* gives direc-

tion to every incident and complication leading to it. Resolution of problem must seem inevitable. Examples of *climax* and *ending* to illustrate confession "take-away."

7 ***Know Your Tools***   **47**
Craftsmanship, specialized application of crafting tools to the Confession. *Transitions* of time, place and action. *Flashbacking*, the technique for sorties into past, similar to forward movement of transitions. Examples of *full, fragmentary* and *double flashback*. *Imagery*, a touch of it does a lot for any confession. *Scenes,* don't duck them — reader wants to see action "on camera." *Foreshadowing* should only tip the lid enough to stir reader's curiosity and imagination. *Plants* — technique similar to foreshadowing, but the purpose is different. *Confession language* — mechanics of it as important as the words. *Talk,* don't *write* the Confession.

8 ***The Word Is . . .***   **58**
Eight elements necessary to every confession — Motivation, Identification by reader, Reality, Action, Conflict, Lesson to be learned, Emotion, Sincerity. Spelled confessionally, *the word is* M-I-R-A-C-L-E-S; measure your story against it.

9 ***Better Sure Than Sorry***   **76**
Research can't be shrugged off. If anything is presented *as* a fact, you can't take factual license with it. Most likely questions of law. Family doctor a prime source of medical information. Regional research is three-fourths the writer's own perceptiveness, and a memory-bank to draw upon. Ordinary little things to make an occupation real. Use of public library, and recommended reference books. "Don't take first authoritative word as the last."

10   *What Happens At Your Typewriter*   87
Every story individual; every writer's view of its problem individual too. You, your theme, and available material determine category — *Family, Documentary, Inspirational* or *Tabloid*. Think of your story as a *whole* right from start. The FIVE STAGES in writing a confession.

11   *Genesis of a Confession*   96
Idea for the story analyzed in Chapter XII came in two parts, with nearly three years between. How it developed. Use of questions and answers — *cause* and *effect* — to build story. Problems and hurdles encountered, and working them out.

12   *Confession Workshop*   101
Reprint of published story. Marginal references to principles, confession elements and crafting tools used. Wrap-up discussion.

13   *Small Packages*   135
The mini-confession. What it is. Editorial value. Source of idea for *Workshop* story in Chapter XIV. Developing clutter of unrelated memories into short-short with significance and *reader identification*. Differences in technique between standard length confession and the "mini."

14   *Mini-Confession Workshop*   139
Reprint of published story with marginal notes for study of principles involved. Wrap-up analysis of how *theme* was focused without "preaching."

15   *Marketing*   149
Areas and factors that remain fairly constant. What rights do you sell? Does endorsing the check cut off chance of "residual goodies"? The foreign markets — sources of information; to sell, watch your

idiom. Agent or direct submission? Delayed reports — should you query? Postal information. Acceptable subjects, range and taboos. Story lengths and rates. Check list of most common reasons for rejects.

16 *Confessioneer's Scrapbag* *157*
Quotes for inspiration, ideas, and just laughs. Tips and miscellaneous techniques. Answers to some of the puzzling questions a confession writer runs up against.

Introduction

How did I get started on confessions? I've often been asked that, sometimes with a down-the-nose inflection, sometimes with the eager seeking out of knowledge that's characteristic of serious writers. The first I have long since learned to brush aside, my answer only a part of the true reason — that *sinning in print pays off*.

Actually, however, back in 1948 I was trying to find where I belonged in the writing field, what market I'd have the best chance of breaking into. So, I set myself a quota of twelve yarns aimed at one specific type of magazine. If I hadn't sold by the twelfth, then I would move on to another group and do twelve more, repeating the process until I'd found the right one for me. And because a very wise professional (who knew no more about the confession than I did at the time) felt that my writing was too inhibited, he advised starting with confessions to "loosen up." A good point, but the wrong concept of the genre.

My eighth confession story sold on its first time out, but by then the plus values of this market had become apparent, and I doubt that I'd have dropped out of it with a twelfth rejection. Because, even though money is delightfully corrupting, there's more to writing than the pay alone. There has to be, or the writing itself will lack the very qualities that pay off. So, this book is my answer to all writers who really want to know, not how I got started doing confessions, but how they can, too. That's the purpose of it. To explain the basic principles, and talk out the problems of writing the modern confession. And to do it as if we were sitting across the table from each other, sharing what every writer dearly loves, the give and take of shoptalk.

In the chapters ahead, we'll examine the individual vertebrae of all creative writing as applied to the specialized first person problem story. How to start a confession, and how to carry it through to a satisfying conclusion. How to make use of your own experiences, and beliefs. How to take an insignificant event, and make it significant, meaningful. How to develop *confession tone,* and how to get *reader identification.*

We'll go into the documentary, the inspirational, the family story, and the increasingly important area of permissiveness, or the so-called "new morality." Occasionally, too, we may pause to listen to a tip from some selling writer (but no names, please — this an anonymous field).

Interested?

Then let me make a few suggestions before we get started. *The Confession Writer's Handbook* is intended to be read clear through as you would a favorite magazine. Don't try to absorb all the principles set forth in this first reading. Instead, lay the book aside for awhile. Later, when you have time, read it again. Now, however, concentrate on the points brought out, chapter by chapter.

You'll find the basic rules are gone into repeatedly, and these repetitions are intentional, since every element of the confession is dependent on all the others, and none can be examined separately without the interaction between them.

When you finish the second reading, start writing. Refer back to appropriate chapters whenever necessary, but the important thing from this point on will be to WRITE. WRITE. WRITE.

Because confessions are deceptively simple, not even the most experienced writer can just sit down to the typewriter and dash one off the first try. I learned by trial and error, and like my own narrators, suffered in the doing. If there had been someone I could've turned to with the countless questions that plagued me, someone to explain how "confessing" differs from any other form of short fiction and why rejection is the penalty of not knowing the answers, my early sins in this highly specialized market might have been easier to overcome.

So, as one writer to another, let's take a look at the Confession. . . .

Chapter One

In the beginning . . .

The line between slicks and confessions is now only a hair's breadth, but like Joseph's Coat, the confession story is of many colors — and fabrics. Some cheap and shoddy, some of the finest quality. In general, this wide variation is due to three factors: hybrid origin, anonymity, and the attitude of writers. Each is woven so tightly into the confession's past, the pattern of its future must also be loomed from the same threads. Before studying confession technique, therefore, you should understand the background of today's liveliest short fiction market.

Back in 1919, *Physical Culture,* a lusty "muscle and carrot" health journal, was receiving mail by the truckload. Flabby-biceped clerks, frustrated wives or husbands, acne-tortured adolescents, all wrote to *PC*, baring their problems as they would to a Father Confessor.

Bernard Macfadden, its publisher, disliked any waste, yet those cries for help, coming straight from the heart of America's reading public, were daily carted off to the city dump. So, it's a fifty-fifty guess whether Scotch thrift, or editorial vision, actually fathered the Confession. At any rate, determined to make use of *Physical Culture's* bulging mail sacks, Mr. Macfadden conceived the idea for a new type of magazine in which he promised to print only authenticated factual experiences, told in the first person by those who had lived through them. As a result, the first issues of *True Story* were hardly more than a compilation of readers' letters, lacking the drama and excitement to hold a mass circulation once the novelty wore off.

Meanwhile, out west in Minneapolis, the Fawcett brothers had struck publisher's gold almost as soon as they climbed out of their doughboy uniforms. Having gathered a plentiful supply of barracks humor while in the army, they were now distributing it to the home front in the pocket-sized monthly, *Captain Billy's Whiz Bang*.

It was a smash hit, and provoked as big a howl from parents as the *new morality* does today. So, with money from sales rolling in faster than it could be banked, and having seen copies of Macfadden's thriving *True Story*, Billy Fawcett decided that he'd try a similar "without benefit of byline" fatherhood.

Aware that the format of such a magazine must necessarily differ from that of a joke book, he prudently asked the University of Minnesota's Department of Journalism for advice. The educators did even better, they loaned him a young honor student, Cecil Pease, and she thereby became the founding editor of *True Confessions*.

According to Mrs. Cecil Pease Webber, the editorship was a complex, and often almost impossible assignment. Contributor, re-write man, make-up chief, trouble-shooter, Madam Editor—and a constant, vigilant watchdog against Captain Billy's whiz-banging into her carefully planned pages, she apparently managed all of it competently, because the first issue sold out within a few hours of hitting the stands.

The fifty odd years since *True Story* and *True Confessions* were thus sired have had their share of hardships, but from them has grown the mature, highly specialized market that today guides millions of readers to a better adjusted, happier way of life.

Confession editors *care* — deeply and sincerely — about their readers, not as faceless figures on a sales chart, but as fellow human beings. That's the inner core of the confession's achievement, the intangible that has earned these first-person books a unique place in the publishing trade.

Of course, the original concept that *this is my honest-to-God story right to the very last comma* was a pledge that couldn't be fulfilled. Long, rambling reports of bona fide, personal sufferings had as little entertainment value as a trip to the corner grocery, and to maintain reader appeal, re-writes were a must. This editorial compromise demanded professionally written stories, based on truth (rather than being word-for-word true) dealing with a common problem developed through incidents that could logically be expected to happen under similar circumstances.

But at the start, established professionals shied away from confession magazines, which was quite understandable. Rates were extremely low then, the scope was limited, and by-lines strictly taboo. Mostly, if freelancers submitted to the market at all, it was as a pot-boiler outlet. So, from the editor's angle, it was a case of being damned if he did, and damned if he didn't — stick to the truth, that is!

During the flaming twenties of the confession's birth, therefore, and on through the depression years, idea merchants provided an emergency source of material. Housewives and businessmen, gifted with an active imagination, peddled capsule plots and ideas for a few dollars apiece — magazine staffs stretching them to story length. These idea merchants were never writers in any real sense, but in their own minds, they've had hundreds of stories published.

"I quit years ago—" they'll glibly impress wide-eyed tyros. "Writing that kind of stuff just isn't worth it!"

The phrase "years ago" is the giveaway of their literary status, and their hundreds of stories don't add up to one legitimate sale, either in dollars or wordage. But let the retired idea merchants enjoy their tiny spotlight if they will—the market outgrew them those same many "years ago"!

It took the confessions more than two decades, however, to outgrow a formula and a gimmick. The narrator had to *sin, suffer and repent* a tear-soaked way through every yarn, or there was no sale. This obviously hobbled creativity. And the gimmick? That was the over-used device of SEX. The knowledge, or understanding of its force in our everyday life was treated in the same manner that a healthy male curiosity went unsatisfied back in Victorian days. In other words, while a man might watch a lady move across the room, *what* caused her to move remained forever unseen!

But with a gradual bettering in rates, skilled writers began to submit, and by the time G.I.'s of the Second World War came home, confession magazines were stylistically far superior to early issues. Editors of the twelve or fifteen books then circulating had even started to probe the potential of the *why* of personal behavior.

Would an emphasis on *why* people behave as they do accomplish more than the *sin, suffer and repent* formula? Would a determined drive to clean up story lines lose what sex and thrills had gained?

That marked the beginning of a new confession — the helping hand offered some friend who faces a crisis, the open assumption of responsibility for a reader's welfare. For the second time, *True Story* broke trail, many of its stories verging on slick quality. Other magazines soon followed that lead. Passion was toned down to emotion, thrills smoothed into drama, and character flaws replaced sin entirely, or else served as the springboard into an expertly analyzed reason for it.

Then, in the late 40's the publishing world was rocked on its collective heels — *Television!* With each new set installed, periodical sales were lost, and frenzied efforts made to restore them to a profitable level. Editors were changed between press runs, blatant sex was re-injected in the confessions, story contests promoted, rates boosted to keep proven writers from bolting to the new medium — and in spite of every stratagem, TV continued to threaten established markets.

One day, after listening to a friend wail about the situation until I'd turned a deep shade of indigo myself, I happened to recall my family's favorite anecdote about a seafaring uncle.

It was a particularly rough voyage in Alaskan waters, and a nervous passenger had approached him. "Won't this storm ever get over, Captain?" she asked fearfully.

Feet planted solidly on the pitching deck, eyes calm and untroubled, he answered simply, "It always has, ma'am — it always has!"

And as far as confessions were concerned, the storm was weathered once they started giving the public what it wanted — just a good story with emotional impact, told by a problem-harried person who might be their own next-door neighbor. Or themselves. The modern confession is actually a first-person human behavior yarn, and makes use of every accepted principle of basic story structure. But it highlights theme and incident more than the slick does, and insists on a lesson to be learned by the reader. Otherwise, the main difference is a matter of subtlety, the confession being more outspoken and with strong reader identification.

It's an emerging market, still plenty rough at times, and still with shoddy magazines on the stands. But on the whole, rather than equating sex with sin, confessions recognize that there is much more to life than sex transgressions, and that a wrong based on other characteristics of the human family can make for a lot of misery, too.

While the moral tone is as high as ever, the facts of life are not ignored, nor our changing attitudes toward them. Although the confession may sometimes look into problems its readers are embarrassed to talk openly about to others, since May, 1919, when the first *True Story* went on sale, the premise that *one person's confession is another's help* has always been the reason for being of every first-person problem story written, just as the six major requirements laid out by Bernard Macfadden remain the same. He demanded — as today's confession editors still do — that these narratives must be (1) completely sincere, (2) true to life, (3) realistic, (4) told in simple, homely language, (5) narrated in the first-person, and (6) must teach a strong moral lesson.

They've come a long way, far beyond what Bernard Macfadden and the Fawcett brothers even dared dream — legitimatized by the prestigious *Wall Street Journal* in a front page feature; a college credit course on confession writing included in the University of Southern California's curriculum; Emory University's School of Medicine publishing its own confession magazine to make medical procedures less frightening to clinic patients; a confession story from the pages of *True Love* awarded the 1972 fiction prize by the National Federation of Press Women; and ten million copies of the confession magazines bought monthly for family reading.

While the exact number shifts slightly year to year, currently there are thirty-eight monthlies and bi-monthlies in publication, including the pioneer *True Story* and *True Confessions*. All reflect the influence of those three factors I mentioned earlier, but while their *hybrid origin* can't be swept under the literary rug, and *anonymity* may always carry some taint of license, the changed *attitude* of those directly involved in their production has given us a new confession — a market in which professional and hobbyist alike can now write with pride and profit.

Chapter Two

The What and The Who

Confessions, like people, are too multi-faceted to fit neatly into any single category. They struggle and dangle and overlap. But in a rough sort of way, most of them can be classified under one of the following:

The Family Problem Story. This is the most generally used type, providing strong reader identification with the narrator's problem, and the environment in which he or she lives.

The Inspirational Story. In this, the narrator overcomes some great handicap, either physical or spiritual, and in so doing inspires the reader to believe that *God's in His heaven, and all's right with the world.*

The Documentary. Advances in medicine and how to cope with sicknesses of various sorts are the most common areas covered here — mental illness, pregnancy and old wives' tales, stroke, the retarded child, seizures such as epilepsy, and so forth — but whatever the problem explored, it is thoroughly documented and backed up by the latest authoritative information available.

The Tabloid. These tend to the lurid, dealing with the more sensational problems that face us today, and have less reader identification than the other categories. They require considerable skill in the writing, are less readily salable, and are used for "right now" timeliness, as well as their sensationalism.

But whatever the category, the reader must be able to feel the reality of it, that it's *a capsule of life worth the reliving,* as John O'Hara once defined the short story. And this is an inflexible rule of the confessional form of the short story — it can be lived in the sense that each is in the realm of the possible. Because millions of housewives, school girls, working women, and a surprising number of men regularly read the first-person problem story for information and guidance, as well as entertainment.

Formerly a tear-drenched carbon copy of a terrible crisis in the narrator's life, confessions have swung over now to a searching into and understanding of human behavior. Just as the doctor has a better chance to cure physical disease if he knows the causes, and psychiatrists often dig back into childhood for the reasons of a psychosis, so the confession writer must be able to analyze motivating causes, and relate them to the effect, or problem of the narrator.

So, *why* is your keyword to the modern confession, and its aim (hopefully, at least) is to reassure the reader that she doesn't walk alone, that you too have faltered, made foolish mistakes, and found a way to lick your problems. You see, the confession reader wants to know that heaven is still operating full time, and to err need not be a one-way ticket to hell.

But, and this is important, you don't offer reassurance by saying, "Just do like I did, and everything will work out fine for you too." The confession is not a neatly packaged tonic for another's ailment, nor is it *add water and mix advice.*

I used to think of confessions as the "couch in print" until a few years ago when I did a lot of research into the Peace Corps, most of it the hard way. From my experience then, I've come to see what a confession really is, a paper and printer's ink counterpart of the Peace Corps Volunteer in action.

Why? Well, the PCV in serving people of under-developed nations shares the same basic aim and methods of reaching them as the fictional housewife telling how she took a job to buy nicer things for the house — and found unhappily that a combination freezer, or 24-inch color TV doesn't automatically make her house a better home.

Exploring the analogy a little further, when a PCV boils drinking water, builds a latrine and whitewashes dirt-encrusted walls of an adobe hut, he follows accepted health rules. And he hopes the other fellow will be stimulated enough by the resultant benefits to think out for himself how to do something about his own sanitation problems.

What I'm getting at is that the confession narrator, if she's worth an editorial nod, also *helps others help themselves,* which is the guiding principle of the Peace Corps — and of today's confession market.

It's no longer that old *sin, suffer and repent* formula — instead, the cause and effect of one person's reaction to a problem is gone into in depth. To do this, you as the writer must participate actively, or as Mark Twain advised, "Don't look at the world with your hands in your pockets — to write about it, you have to reach out and touch it."

To reach out and touch life, this is what the confession does. It meets the problems of everyday life squarely, and wrestles with them. But why not tell your story the same as any other, rather than a person-to-person confidence? Marriage counsellors and psychiatrists agree that the talking out of a problem leads to its solution. The Roman Catholic Church, too, has always urged members to bare their innermost thoughts and mistakes to a Father Confessor, offering them the anonymity of a curtained confessional booth.

In other words, people need to talk to someone who will

understand, and they don't want to do it where the whole town will know who is doing the talking — this is the theory of a confession story, the secret of its success.

Of course, writing for the confessions will never have the prestige of a byline in the *Atlantic Monthly,* nor the status of big-name slicks. But ask yourself this — why am I writing, is it to impress the neighbors, to be Harriet Hemline, the Author? If the answer is *yes,* forget the confession market, it offers you nothing.

There are many kinds of writers though, and not all of us have the right genes to produce a salable confession story. I don't mean to lay it on with a heavy and dedicated hand, but you must be a rather special sort of person to write and sell these yarns with any consistency. Special, and even a little strange!

First, you must have a split personality — split a hundred different ways. So, let's start off by answering a few questions:

1. Forget what your education may be, just tell me this — can you work with characters that are mixed-up, torn by conflicting emotions, and blind to their own besetting faults?

2. Do you have the compassion to understand these characters of your own imagination, and the wisdom to see a solution to their problems when none seems possible?

3. Can you make this one person's experience universal? Can you live his or her life during a significantly difficult period in such a way that thousands, perhaps even millions, of other people are able to identify with that particular problem?

You see, these qualities are essential to the confession writer, and you either have them, or you don't. But everything else can be learned, and two-thirds of it lies in the basic principles of all short fiction, together with an understanding of the Three Unities — unity of time, place and action.

The other third — what makes the Confession different — is where so many writers fail, largely because its elements are those of any short story, but their application is purely confessional in treatment. While the technique of this, too, can be learned, you must be prepared to spend considerable time at your typewriter before the necessary *confession tone* is finally achieved. On the other hand, if you've answered the three questions above in the affirmative, and are blessed with a plentiful supply of perception, emotion, imagination, compassion, and determination, time and purposeful writing will do the rest.

Now, while this may sound facetious, every confession story must have a *beginning, a muddle, and an ending.* If the problem isn't one that gets the narrator into a real muddle in her impulsive and mistaken attempts to find a way out, there's no object lesson for readers, which is the aim of all confessions. So, a *muddle* is the special catalyst that synthesizes the straight short story to an emotional experience, and through *reader identification,* helps others to help themselves.

And since it's important that you, as Pygmalion to your narrator's Galatea, aren't muddled too, you'd do well to memorize this fit-all pattern for short stories, and then we can put in the tucks or needed darts that will adjust it to the confession:

1. What does the narrator want? (Problem)
2. What prevents her getting it? (Complication)
3. What does she do about this obstacle? (Conflict)
4. What are the results of what she does? (The Muddle)
5. What show-down does all of it lead to? (The Dark Moment)
6. Does she get what she wants, or doesn't she? (Resolution)

7. What have I been saying? (Theme)
8. Finally, what is the "take-away"? (Lesson to be learned)

So, confessions, just as any other short fiction, start with the viewpoint character — the narrator — facing a problem that concerns her more than anybody else, and which must be resolved in the immediate future, although the effects on her life are long-range. But she has a character flaw, or mistaken attitude, which causes her to persist in making the wrong decision. By so doing, she brings down tragedy (comparative in relation to seriousness of the problem) on herself, or loved ones.

Once the narrator sees where she's been wrong, she sets about rectifying the mistake as far as possible. And if you let your protagonist see the cause, and how her earlier action has set the wheels of tragedy in motion but she can't stop them, it'll be a better confession. In any event, she'll always make the wrong decision first, and because of it, trouble results. She then fumbles and muddles her own way back through new complications to a logical solution, and a ray of hope for the future if she's learned the lesson your story exemplifies.

To bring this about believably, you should know the ending of your confession from the start in order to give a unified direction, and avoid having to contrive the problem's resolution. Put another way, it simply means that the opening grows from the ending, and how your narrator reacts to the problem determines the complications which lie between, unfolding to a satisfying and inevitable resolution.

But *reader identification* is something else again. It's probably the hardest single essential to master in confession writing — and the most intangible. Yet what creates that same identification is inherent in almost every element of your story — problem, characterization, situation, conflict, complication, and the motivating forces to weld them all together.

By focusing on it, therefore, from the moment a story idea is born, you'll create that necessary rapport between narrator and reader. Myself, I find it helps to think of *reader identification* as a "golden thread" I'm pulling through my story. And if I don't let go of it, the *confession tone* is preserved.

So, as we look at sources of ideas in our next chapter, and how to develop them into salable confessions, concentrate on the "golden thread" for each. It's literally your narrator's lifeline, because without a tight hold on it, she won't reach print.

Chapter Three

Problem and Theme

Basically, confessions are all *problem* stories, the resolution of which provides a *theme* that gives readers new insight into their own flawed life pattern.

Suppose a neighbor's brother has recently returned from overseas, and he says that thousands of war orphans are starving there. "Isn't it awful—" you'll comment, "poor little things!" And that will be the end of their misery so far as you're concerned.

But if your neighbor, over a cup of coffee, tells you the squalling baby that's kept the whole neighborhood awake is a war orphan brought here by a civilian worker back from Saigon, and there hasn't been a drop of milk in its mouth all week, you're stirred to action, aren't you?

Hunger is still the problem, yet no longer that of faceless thousands starving in a far off land. You can walk across the street, knock on the door, and see this starving baby with your own eyes. Its pitiful condition is real, and you're impelled to do something at once. And snap decisions tend to be trouble makers!

So, now we know that even though the *problem* must be common to people everywhere, a confession is the story of one person made vulnerable to its bedevilment through immediate circumstances, and a mistaken attitude or character flaw. Your choice of that problem is as wide as the world you live in — deeply touching, sensational, or perhaps just the frustration of a young wife who wants nicer things for her family on a no-stretch budget.

The girl whose parents have stayed together "for the children's sake," determines that she won't be similarly trapped by marriage. Instead, she'll live by her own terms — sex, but no emotional entanglement. That problem has been used, and will be used again and again. So has the philandering husband, and the teenager who compromises with honesty to get accepted by the "right crowd." In fact, it's impossible to come up with an original problem. No matter what your choice, someone, somewhere, will have already used it for a confession. But you can reach print if your approach is fresh, or focused from a different angle.

The subject of blindness, for instance, has been overworked. But what about the plain-Jane who marries a blind man? To her husband's sensitive touch she is thrillingly beautiful, so when an experimental and extremely risky surgical technique offers him an outside chance to see again, the narrator is faced with disaster. An interesting twist, isn't it — the wife who wants a handicapped husband?

When you have explored the possibilities of a problem, and have come up with an approach that seems fresh, make sure it has sufficient emotional potential to result in a furious struggle, both within and without the narrator. Because, no matter how important the problem, or how fresh your approach, if it's too easily resolved, readers aren't going to care one way or the other. And unless they do, you've failed in the confession's purpose.

Problems that pass along helpful information on medical advances, or show up old wives' tales for what they are, sell readily. The varied problems of a man-woman relationship — and these aren't limited to just a sexual aspect — are generally money in the bank, too. So is bigotry and prejudice, if you stay off the soap box, although it was just beginner's luck that I managed to in my first confession. I still have the letter from Hazel Berge, then the editor of *Modern Romances*, complimenting me on "the discreet and subtle handling of a very delicate subject."

Actually, I hadn't thought of it as a racial story. I'd known a light-complected black girl in high school who attempted "passing" as white, and the conflict she must've felt within herself kept nagging at me until I finally wrote her story. The secret of the success of "Count Romance Out" was that I didn't preach or crusade, I simply told her story!

That same problem is the basis for many of today's confessions, varying only as the theme changes. *You can't run away from yourself, Honesty is the best policy, What you are inside is what counts,* and maybe a dozen more could be the lesson a bi-racial girl learns. But whatever your theme, don't state it outright — *theme* should be implicit in the story.

And no matter how trite and worn, you can breathe freshness into your theme by keeping in mind that no two people are ever exactly alike, nor any two problems identical. We each react to a given situation in a different way — we fight, we cajole, or we cry ourselves out of trouble according to our individual natures. And because we each are motivated differently, the truth we learn in the doing differs, too.

There is only one rule I have for writing confessions: *The problem's solution is the logical and inevitable result of all that has gone before, and must always exemplify the theme that the build-up of the problem has developed.* In other words, *problem* and *theme* are inseparable.

So, where do you find themes? Well, Aesop's Fables are literally a gold mine to the confession writer. Remember the dog that saw his own reflection in the water, and lost the bone he carried by trying to grab the reflected bone too

— how many modern stories are written around the theme of *Greed can cost your all?*

Proverbs like *Pride goeth before a fall, It's always darkest before the dawn,* and *Happiness cannot be bought* show up time and again as confession themes.

The Bible, too, is one of our best sources of theme. With no irreverence meant, *The Prodigal Son* is one of the greatest confession stories ever told. So is *The Story of Ruth,* and *Jeptha's Daughter,* or *Cain and Abel.*

Actually, however, expressing *theme* in a single sentence is only a useful guideline to the writer. Because, deep down, the confession's theme is so closely related to every other element, it can't be stated except in terms of the story as a whole. You see, it's never imposed on the material, but grows out of it, with action and dialogue *creating,* not illustrating, the lesson to be learned.

We must create living people to meet our chosen confession problem head-on, or it's only a few sheets of wasted bond — just "dry bones" that good *characterization* would've made come alive. So, that's what we are going to talk about next . . .

Chapter Four

Characterization

"Your plot must always come first —" there's no way to know how many writers have been blocked by that dictum. Certainly I was, but before the block became chronic, an old pro showed the fallacy up for what it really is.

"Take *Gone with the Wind,* can you give me its plot?" he asked, nodding when I could only say it was some sort of a Civil War story. "Don't remember how it goes, hmm — well, what about Scarlett O'Hara and Rhett Butler?"

Two questions, and with them he handed me a writing tool that's been invaluable. Because Rhett and Scarlett were still as sharply vivid in my mind as when I'd laid the book down, while details of the story they had lived were faded into a shadowy limbo.

Plot — the Miss Thistlebottoms of the literary world have made a holy cow of *plot,* just as they sanctify the unsplit infinitive. Yet to take the opposite view, and insist that *plot* is only a pattern cut by the people it clothes, and secondary to character, is equally fallacious. You must have both, and both are on the same level of importance. With a thin or hackneyed plot, problem and theme are weakened. And the strongest plot will seem contrived unless the characterization is solid.

If you have an especially big problem getting past that four-letter block, try substituting the words *road map* for *plot!* While this may sound like over-simplification, even silly, I discovered long ago that it works. But before we go into the purpose of plotting, let's discuss the confessional approach to characterization.

Since there must be no sense of the fictional in these stories, confessions don't sell easy solutions, or guarantee happiness — they show *people adjusting to situations.* Flesh and blood people, with a narrator readers will care about, seeing their faults reflected in hers. So, to breathe life into confession characters, we must recognize that they have traits, just as you and I do. Because we all share the same essential hopes and fears — the nagging anxieties, the struggle for money, for love, and the daily difficulty of communicating with another human being — something of ourselves goes into each confession we write. If it doesn't, our characters are mere images, rolled flat by a typewriter platen.

I remember a woman who tried confessions some years ago. She had a lively imagination and a way with words, but her stories lacked the reader sympathy that's a must.

"I will not expose myself — it's not necessary," she insisted. "An intelligent person can write a convincing story by the proper choice of words, and application of basic principles."

Stubbornly, she refused to probe into her own heart and emotions, or to experience them again on paper. Even a little trick I'd found useful in my early days was rejected because, "Some things are too personal to spread around," including uninhibited letters that wouldn't be mailed after their writing.

Now, although I promised not to burden you with rules, I've been sneaky and used this anecdote to underscore an imperative no confession writer can afford to skirt — *you and your narrator are inseparable; your innermost thoughts, emotions, and memories give life to hers.* That's the secret of characterizing in the confessions, so keep it in mind, and we'll examine some of the many lives of a confessioneer.

Myself, I find friends the best source of story people. But wait — that doesn't mean using them in my stories, except as a key to unlock character. I take somebody whose nature might cause her to react in a certain way to certain situations. Knowing this person, I can logically project the effect of such conflict so that there'll be a transferral of reality to my narrator's collision with the story problem, and its eventual resolution. In fact, my own identification is so strong, I've sometimes found it necessary to use her true name in first drafts. An instance of that was a story I'd started at least a half dozen times only to have the narrator woodenly immovable unless I pulled the strings. Finally, I changed her name to *Ruthie,* and she immediately came alive. My story did too!

But if you must resort to the same device, be sure to change the name back again before submission. Because your narrator won't be the person you started out with, nor the resultant confession her story. The mechanical use of the name merely serves as a kind of catalyst to transform ribbon-ink to the warm flow of blood through that character's veins.

And while we're on names, take care their choice doesn't become just a handy *pencil sharpener.* We all have plenty of reasons to procrastinate without adding another, and if a name grates or seems dated generation-wise, the editor will change it to a more suitable one.

My point here, however, is that the name should *feel* right to you while the story is in your typewriter. Otherwise, you'll probably have to force characters to perform, and once you start that, the illusion of reality won't come across. So, make use of any device which aids you, as a writer, to achieve this essential quality.

That's the primary purpose of confession characterization, to help readers identify with the people inhabiting a story, those who motivate or experience its plot-action, and who prove out the theme it illustrates.

To accomplish this, you must believe in your characters yourself, because when they're real to the writer, convincing others of their reality is much easier.

There will, of course, be times when characters are wholly fabricated, but you still must know those persons intimately, or their characterization will be as thin as the air they come from. They should be fixed in your own mind in sufficient depth to understand what makes them tick. Their background, their origins, their beliefs, should be clearly defined. Their basic wants, and needs and emotions should be apparent. You should establish what they look like, how they think and act, be aware of their personality quirks. In substance, you must have at your fingertips — literally so — all the attributes that combine to make up the individual character, and distinguish him or her from every other person in your confession.

And don't depend on a general knowledge of human behavior for this. Instead, even though it takes time and effort, you'll find a fully written profile of each key character pays off in a deeper understanding of your story people, which activates that vital pulse of life-giving blood.

The profile, therefore, should be a complete dossier dealing with the genesis, personality traits, drives and ambitions, family background, physical description, and character-building or warping events that contribute to a specific pattern of behavior. Once you have this detailed information down on paper, classified as indicated in part here, be selective. Determine which traits you're going to emphasize, which conditioning events in the character's emotional or physical past will best motivate action and reaction within the plot pattern. Which characteristics you'll actually use in the story itself. The rest is that old seven-eighths of the iceberg again — there, just not seen openly.

But won't pinning characters to paper like this hamper creativity? Let me answer that with another question, does knowing the real person a character is drawn from bind you creatively? Well, the study and absorbing of biographical data contained in such profiles is merely the careful writer's method of getting to *know* a character so thoroughly he can, for all practical purposes, become that story person. Then, rather than creating an emotional response to any given circumstance or situation, he'll experience it — and the reader will too.

You see, readers want to feel, to be moved emotionally, and *the foundation of all emotional response is characterization*. But, and watch this, *caring* is the one emotion toward which every other emotion is built. So, if the reader doesn't care that Midge Hendron quits her job, or that the Carmichael's baby is born blind, it's because she hasn't been given the wherewithal to identify with them. They aren't story people, and no amount of dramatic events is going to pump life into such author-manipulated puppets!

The important thing, therefore, is to keep in mind that the majority of confession readers are much the same as ourselves. Ordinary people living ordinary lives — housewives, blue collar workers, stenos, store clerks, community college students, young professionals just starting out — the broad middle level of Americans. That's where your narrator belongs, not in the Jet Set, or on welfare. But she still won't come across unless she's living in a real world, with everybody in it flesh and blood too, right down to the most minor character.

I read a friend's confession recently which revolved around a problem child, the three-year old son of the husband's army pal whom they have taken in until an adoptive home can be found. They shower love and affection on the little orphan, but are met with hostility and tantrums. Finally, ready to climb the wall, the narrator spanks him — and that's it! The boy is tractable at last, and recalling her mother's strictness, she realizes that "Mom" had *cared enough to discipline her.* The trouble is, all we have is one sentence early in the story that "Mom" was stern and seemingly unloving, so when she resolves her own problem the same way, it's contrived and the theme doesn't ring true.

To my friend, the narrator's mother was never a real person, just a prop she dragged in for that later purpose, meanwhile completely overlooking her *in a way no one in real life can be overlooked.* Characterizing those who influence the viewpoint character's actions, then, you actually give depth to her as an individual. But don't let the reader be aware of what you're doing — always weave in whatever information is necessary to understand character, motivation and situation as part of the forward moving story-action.

Once you have an individual in mind, you're faced next with having to get him or her across to readers, and in the confessions, dialogue and action are the most effective means for this. Suppose your narrator is married to a country doctor who puts healing ahead of fees, "and if somebody who'd never paid him a dime woke up with heartburn at two o'clock in the morning, he was on his way regardless."

> Okay, I admit fresh eggs and country sausage and bushel baskets of rosy-cheeked Gravenstein apples are fine. We could use them, but we could use money better and more often. I remember once Ken brought home a shabby, old paisley shawl that Mrs. Robertson had given him for pulling her little boy through a near fatal siege of pneumonia.
>
> "Is that all your time and medical know-how is worth?" I'd exploded. "Is that what she calls a

fee for saving her youngster's life? That won't pay our bills!"

"It belonged to her great-grandmother, honey!" he said softly, and folded the shawl carefully away on the top closet shelf.

While characterization is continuous, and should never be presented in one indigestible chunk, still even these few lines out of context tell us quite a bit about the narrator's doctor-husband. Like doing more than lip service to the Hippocratic Oath, his compassion, and how he can appreciate a *Gift of Love*.

None of that is said?

No, not in so many words, but read the excerpt through again, and I think you'll catch my point. Readers don't want to be told what a character is, they want to see for themselves. When Ken says softly that the faded old paisley shawl had belonged to Mrs. Robertson's great-grandmother, "and folded it carefully away on the top closet shelf," the reader takes accurate measure of this man.

Everything done, every reaction, every word spoken should be chosen to convey the person's character and personality, and here's where one-liner characterizations are invaluable. Without any break in pace, a few words imply the dominant trait of a character, yet a great deal more is revealed between the lines.

The example above is, of course, "loaded." Besides characterizing Ken, *problem* and *theme* are indicated, and another important aid to characterization is there too. *Symbols*. When I was very small my Irish grandmather told me that stars are the holes angels poke in the floor of heaven so they can keep watch over us. I used that to symbolize "love never gets lost" in my story about an airline stewardess who falls in love with a pilot.

After awhile it got so Johnny and flying and the

stars were all mixed together in my faith and inner beliefs . . .

She says that when they flew straight toward the stars, it was like reaching out to touch the hand of a special friend, and on a night flight once, she'd mentioned how Gram had called them "holes in the floor of heaven."

"There, that big one up near the Dipper —" Johnny suddenly exclaimed, "That's our star, Chris baby — it's big enough so a guy could look over the angel's shoulder, and see the whole works down on earth!"

His arm tightened, and he swung me around to face him. "I love you Chris," Johnny whispered tenderly. "I'll never stop loving you as long as I live — or afterward either!"

That last foreshadows Johnny's later death in a plane crash, and the star *that's big enough so a guy could look over the angel's shoulder* plays a significant part in her eventual adjustment to his loss — and does it with no sense of contriving or credibility gap, when she finds it possible to "pick up the pieces and look ahead, not back. To take the past and build the future from it!"

Search your own memory and experience for homely bits of philosophy, family sayings, customs, beliefs, the sparrow with a broken wing, the golden glory that's hidden within the browned husk of a daffodil bulb, or the unbroken circle of an old fashioned wedding band. These are *symbols* that can be used to bring out the inner self of a confession character, their very familiarity making it easier for readers to understand and like her, even while disapproving of what she does. Because no matter how mixed up the narrator is, no matter how far she strays from accepted moral standards, she must be likable — or no sale.

Oddly, however, it's easier to develop an unsympathetic character than one the reader cares about. Don't ask me why, it just is. But she can't be "sugar and spice, and everything nice" either. Remember, the narrator is a real person, and therefore, full of human frailties too. Let her scream at the children, burn the stew, and sometimes hold out grocery money for an expensive lipstick when a dime store one would serve as well. We all do things like that, and so will any confession character who's worth an editorial nod.

Even so, certain unlikable narrators show up frequently, and are rejected with equal frequency. Henry Malmgreen, editing *Modern Romances,* identified the more common of these confessional misfits in one of his *Newsletters.*

Narrators the confession editor doesn't want to meet

Dora The Doormat. She takes it and takes it and takes it — from husband, sweetheart, parents, everyone she comes in contact with. Oh, she complains plenty, but she never does anything about it. Or if she finally takes positive action, it is so late in the story that she's already lost most of her readers.

Stupid Sally. She's a sweet kid, but she doesn't know enough to pound sand in a rat hole. Give her a choice of men, and she'll unerringly pick the one who will devote his life to making her miserable. When she has rushed into marriage without thought of the consequences, and finds that it's not roses, roses all the way, she makes matters worse by getting pregnant — never having heard, apparently, of contraception. Usually she has two or three babies in quick succession and, of course, can't cope with them. Confession readers may not be the most sophisticated people in the world, but they're smart enough to be irritated and bored by this feckless type of narrator.

Neurotic Noreen. This narrator has one fixed idea or attitude that governs all her behavior. It may be grief for her dead child — or devotion to an ailing parent — or resentment of a stepfather — or almost anything that, while natural enough in small doses, is a neurotic symptom when it becomes an obsession. Ordinary, normal people not only don't understand neurotic behavior, they don't particularly want to understand it.

Bossy Beulah, sometimes known as Know-it-all Nellie. Usually, although not always, this narrator is a mother who just can't keep her cotton-pickin' hands off her child's or her children's affairs. Her intentions, of course, are the best — but you know what good intentions are used for paving. The end of the story always finds her straightening up and flying right — but as with Dora the Doormat, by that time readers just won't care.

Madeline the Martyr. She's a kissing cousin to Dora the Doormat — except while Dora LETS people push her around, Madeline goes out of her way to put herself into situations that will mess up her life. Her parents, siblings, children, or husband don't have to ask Madeline to put her own interests second to theirs — she does it herself, and eagerly. And while confession readers are nice people, capable themselves of unselfish behavior, they aren't superhumanly noble and self-sacrificing — and they can't sympathize with a narrator who is.

Tina the Teen-age Terror. Every time the newspapers come out with some new report of teen-age misdeeds in real life — vandalism, narcotic addiction, sex clubs, whatever — there's a rash of stories based on these news items. Such things happen, don't they? Sure, they do, but adult readers hate the kids who make them happen — and to tell the truth, most teen-age readers hate them too. Any narrator who gets herself involved with such capers is a kid nobody wants to read about. Even if her involvement is relatively innocent (she didn't know the others were that kind), she runs a risk of sounding like Stupid Sally.

Tommy the Tom-cat. He's rough, he's tough, and sex is all he's got in mind. Now, we all know that the sex urge is strong in young males, and that in real life our Tom may not be entirely uncommon. But the point is, again, that regardless of conditions in real life, women DON'T WANT to read about such characters, and won't try to identify with them.

Put these same characters "on the couch" though, and thoughtful analysis will make most of them fit to join their peers in the confession market-place. A thorough understanding of their background and occupation will help. So will being selective in deciding which traits to highlight, and which to suppress.

Never reproduce a person exactly the way he or she is in real life, because the difference between a *real* character and a dramatized character is a necessary difference for "story flow." Most of us, you see, are too complex and contradictory for full detailing. Instead, take one or two dominant characteristics, and focus on them, keeping all the others subordinate. Remember, also, that characters are developed and their traits established by what is going on in the world — we don't live in a vacuum, and neither should your story people.

When you come right down to it, successful characterization in the confessions is *little things used purposefully* — and writing about them from the inside-out.

You may have trouble with it at first. I did, until one scorching day when I'd climbed that endless circular stairway to the top of the Statue of Liberty, and stood looking out across the New York harbor through narrow windows cut into the thick stone wall. Then, happening to glance upward, I saw the rise of a massive arm, saw the torch held aloft in great firm fingers — and knew I was literally seeing the gateway to America through the eyes of Liberty!

I've never forgotten the emotional impact of that winging excitement, and while mine was an actual physical experience, this describes what it means to *climb inside your narrator, and look at the world through her eyes.*

But to manage that feat, you must first know people and fully understand their behavior. In fact, the old Chinese philosopher who said, "Sorrow not that men do not know you, but sorrow that you do not know man," might well have been advising today's confession writer.

Chapter Five

Plot

Plot vs. Characterization — do characters make the story, or is plot the primary consideration? While both notions can be supported by sound reasoning, and are stubbornly debated when the two schools of confession writers get together, that time-battered controversy is actually insoluble. Plot can't come into being without characters to move it, and characters are immobile without plot — neither can function alone.

Keep in mind that confessions are always about believable people doing believable things. Consequently, the building of a plot, and the choosing of characters should be worked out at the same time — if you think of *what* is to happen in the course of action, you must also think of *who* will be involved. Plot and character.

Our own greatest problem at this point, and probably the reason a Thistlebottomish over-emphasis has been placed on it, is plotting. But writers, particularly those who haven't yet discovered the stimulus of craftsmanship, tend to starve their creativity. They get an idea, and seize it as a ready-made story; they snare an incident, and sit back hoping it'll grow Topsy-like into a fully developed yarn. Go at it that way, and you have only yourself to blame for the resultant mental block, the *I can't plot* bugaboo of writers who make something complex out of what's merely the *cause and effect of conflict.*

Now, since conflict obviously powers the confession, the drive which puts the narrator in conflict should be so universal that a strong emotional response is aroused in the reader. Because, once readers care about her, they're drawn into and forward by plot-action.

Your job then, is to see the story problem with human eyes — the narrator's eyes. And we all look at things differently, so the *kind* of person chosen to re-live a certain experience commits the writer to a certain *kind* of emotion, and action, and hope of resolving it.

But the narrator can't stumble along an obstacle course to the problem's resolution, creating incidents helter-skelter out of the special quality of her nature.

When a story germ hits in the guise of an event, therefore, you must at once determine the sort of person to whom it will happen. Because upon that person's character traits depend his reaction, and upon that reaction depends what happens next.

So, ask yourself first why you want to write this particular story — to make a point, tell a meaningful experience, or reveal something? Then, with its purpose clear, you *establish* the narrator's conflict, *dramatize* that conflict, and *resolve* the conflict. This is all plotting really amounts to, just *organized conflict!*

There's more than one way to formulate a plot, however, and until you have found the method that will be most comfortable for you, mine may help. On the psychological principle of a little at a time, I start with four skeletal questions:

1. *WHO* is the protagonist, the narrator who'll best act out the theme my story is to illustrate?
2. *WHY* has the pivotal situation come up, and why

does the narrator react as she does?

3. *HOW* did the problem arise, and how is it brought into focus, causing a forward movement of complications?

4. *WHAT* is the climax, and the problem's resolution?

The answers to these questions are literally the bones of my plot, so I spend considerable time doodling with them until they mesh into what seems a workable combination.

Suppose the situation is a jury fix. I might finally decide the narrator should be a young wife faced by a critical family emergency, and no place to turn for money to handle it. When she's drawn for jury duty just before a sensational murder trial opens, she seems the most vulnerable to bribery, and a cohort of the accused murderer makes contact with her.

An outright offer to buy her verdict, though, will lose reader sympathy if she accepts — if she turns it down, the story ends right there. But a ruse to get the bribe into her possession while the pressures of the family crisis mount, could create a temptation too much for her to handle. What happens in the jury room peaks the conflict within herself, and being the sort of woman she is, the narrator exposes the jury fix.

Too predictable — where's the drama and suspense? Frankly, at this point it's all still in my imagination. But I do know the start and the end of that trip into bribery, so the narrator just needs a *road map* to get her from here to there. And this is how I prefer to think of plot, as a map of the route she will follow.

Using the *what if* method now, I decide on the incident that throws the narrator into conflict, keeping it within the framework of those sketchy answers to my four plot-making questions. The effect of this opening conflict then causes further complications, which in turn will themselves create more conflict. In the process, my imagination begins to work, and I can flesh out the *Who, Why, How* and *What* to synopsis form.

My synopsis is flat, a brief chronological account, intended only to pin the sequence of events in place so that I won't detour from the story line when it comes to the actual writing. But all the action, emotion and characterizing, every dramatic scene and complicating event is there — a word or a sentence covers it. Let me show you what I mean with this excerpt lifted from the synopsis for our bribe-taker's confession:

> Back from the hospital that evening Enid sees ten one-hundred dollar bills on the hall table right where Lee Bradley had laid his brief case earlier. When she phones him, he disclaims ownership — and Enid knows the thousand dollars is a bribe.

So, now we'll look at the scene that's written between those lines, and watch for any straying from them, or the four plot-maker questions which hold the story in line:

> Home again, I switched on the lights and dropped my bag on the hall table. That was when I discovered the money lying there, right where Lee Bradley had set his brief case — ten hundred-dollar bills!
>
> The poor guy must be half out of his mind, wondering where he'd lost it — the crisp bills crackled in my fingers, and for just a moment I matched them against Bill's medical expenses, and the mortgage payments, and all our other debts that had been piling up for almost six months now.
>
> It's not stealing, not really, I thought. But in my heart I knew it would be, and with a sigh, reached for the phone.
>
> "I didn't lose any money," Lee sounded bewildered when I got hold of him.
>
> "Then how —"

"Worry only gets you gray hairs, Enid," he broke in. "Hey, remember what we talked about before — well, everything's okay now!"

And before I could say another word, he'd hung up.

I knew then it was a bribe! Lee had been a go-between, and once he made certain I'd be on the Grainger jury, this thousand dollars showed up out of nowhere.

Well, I was a natural for bribery, wasn't I? "With Bill sick, I'd like anything that pays off in cash," I told Lee the day he drove me home. Still, suppose Pete Grainger really was innocent. . . .

You see, although the synopsis is unhighlighted, it indicates each significant happening, but keeps it in proportion to the whole, with the dramatic conflict of a story unified and clear.

You match, and piece and fit — *if Mary does this, what will Jon do; if this happens, will this other result?*

And when it all fits together, the incidents credibly interlocked and its progression direct, plot is a guideline to keep you going straight ahead from opening to ending.

Myself, I prefer a synopsis to the detailed outline, and not always in writing either, because I feel freer to move around within it, perhaps switching incidents, or dropping in little human interest developments as the story expands on paper. The main thing — whether synopsis or outline — is to have the narrator's course well in mind, and hold her to it.

But whatever your method, once you understand its real purpose, plotting the confession can even be fun!

Chapter Six

Opening and Ending

From a writer's angle, the Opening is probably the most challenging part of any confession. It takes only a minute to read, yet hours — even days — may have gone into its writing. That's because we can no longer take the easy way and just start off *Once upon a time,* letting characters drift in at will, the problem crop up by happenstance, and the resolution a surprise to everyone. Including the writer.

Instead, as in a newspaper lead, the opening paragraphs establish *who, what, why* — and *where* your confession is going. And this last must be known before starting, otherwise the story lacks direction. If it does, you may very well find yourself coming up to the story's end, saddled with a tangential problem which has taken over somewhere along the way.

These 4 W's identify your narrator, present the immediate problem, motivate his or her reaction to it, and lay the groundwork for its eventual resolution. But that's not all the first couple of hundred words do. They set the mood too, foreshadowing the complications ahead, and at least brush in lightly the setting.

The opening, you see, is more than just an interest grabber. It also serves to *prepare* the reader, and requires your fullest attention. And patience. In fact, as a writer friend confessed to me, he once wrote one hundred openings, and finally used No. 35! A lot of work for "just one story"; hardly worth the effort? Well grandmother used to harp that *Anything worth doing is worth doing your best,* and the returns of confession writing, monetarily and craft-wise, are worth everything you put into it. This I can promise you!

There's no fit-all pattern, but as a rule, a story that opens with action has more grab to it than narration. I like to begin with something going on, a scene that takes place at one of three points of time — right *before* the problem arises, when it *actually confronts* the narrator, or *immediately afterward,* making some definite action a necessity. Your choice depends upon the comparative dramatic strength of each, and its action-promoting possibilities.

If you have an idea for a pre-problem scene that does the double job of introducing your narrator interestingly, and emphasizing the brightness of things before the problem arises in sharp contrast to the bleakness afterward, then use it. But keep that pre-problem scene fairly brief, not over 500 words at most. Remember, it's the problem that grips the reader, and she isn't willing to wait too long for trouble to show up.

On the other hand, opening at a high point of suspense will create dramatic action, and background information can then be sifted into the story's forward movement by use of a flashback. But watch this, the flashback *always comes after a dramatic situation, not in the midst of it.* Otherwise, breaking off for a long involved flashback risks the very thing you're trying to do — hook the reader.

And speaking of *hooks,* don't use a grappling hook like the young writer who took "dramatic" to mean *startling* — her opening certainly was all of that!

"Hi, honey — " I called, unlocking our apartment door, "made it back sooner than —"

I broke off, horror washing over me. There in the middle of the living room stood my wife, stark naked. And coming out of the bathroom, his muscular body still wet from the shower, was a man I'd never seen before . . .

That's in the same category as the classic no-no, "Hell —" said the Duchess, "let go of my leg!" Anything following either lead would be an anti-climax. So, dramatic conflict — yes. Shock for shock's sake — no! By way of illustration, compare those two shockers with another opening:

Mama Marino laid the check down beside Jim, and as he reached for his wallet, I glanced casually toward the entrance of the small cafe. Dale — it couldn't possibly be him, yet there he was, a grin tipping his mouth at sight of me.

"Susie —" before I caught my breath, he was at our table. "Lord, gal — it's been years."

"This is my husband, Jim Hunter," somehow I managed to keep my tone light and steady, hoping against hope Dale would have the compassion to take a hint and leave me alone now. "We live here in Astoria, and —"

"Say, aren't you the same Hunter who got elected today for County Commissioner — congratulations!" he broke in, dark eyes pinpointing. "Look, Susie — how about us getting together to hash over old times, hmm?"

Double talk, that's what it was, and underneath his breezy friendliness, I sensed the thin edge of menace.

Don't let him get his scheming fingers around our lives, I prayed, panic trembling along every nerve in me. Don't let him hurt Jim too . . .

There's *conflict* here, and a later crisis is foreshadowed. But when you start at a point of major crisis, you're headed for an anti-climax — or absurdity!

Most of my published yarns open with a provocative situation, although not necessarily a narrative hook in its strictest sense. What makes a provocative situation? Basically, it is something that stirs imagination or curiosity — the writer's way of saying, "This is the situation, and here are the people involved — do you want to know what happens to them?"

Actually, while that handy *Once upon a time* is out nowadays, the words of the old fairy story opening should be there invisibly, overlaid by the typewritten ones which offer a promise, or create a mood. Words that make your reader every bit as eager as the child who can scarcely wait to find out more about *Rapunzel* way up there in her tower.

To see how others have accomplished this, take a current issue of some confession magazine, and type off the openings of each story. Study these for *conflict, suspense, foreshadowing,* and what triggers the complications that follow. Then try an opening of your own — get inside the narrator and present the situation vividly, but with an eye on the story's end. Not the particular incident which closes it, of course, only how the problem is to be resolved. In other words, know where you're going before you start.

Ordinarily, the best way to open is at the beginning of real trouble, using *fragmentary flashbacks* to weave in background and motivation. Sometimes, however, the problem-motivator occurs at a much earlier period. When it does, a *full flashback* is most often used. But the sense of "immediacy" must be maintained then through live-action scenes, not narration, or such necessary information makes dull reading. The alternative to these longer excursions into the past is a *chronological* treatment, the forward movement unbroken by either a full or fragmentary flashback. Instead, if something in the narrator's childhood has caused her motivating character flaw, the story opens at that point. It's tricky though, and dragginess is always a threat.

Your material should determine which of the three formats to use, and the story emphasis will usually indicate the type of opening — atmosphere, dialogue, situation, suspense, or whatever. Just as an example, let's look at a few possibilities:

Situation Opening using fragmentary flashbacks

The wind-whipped hulk of Gull Island had never seemed so grim, and not even crisp white paint, nor the gleaming brass that capped its beacon tower could lighten the gloom.

"Darn it, Dave — I wish we hadn't told him tomorrow is Christmas Day," I swung from the window, eyes brimming. "It's so important to a kid Johnny's age."

"Sure, but there's too much sea running for the boys to risk crossing," he reminded patiently. "As soon as this blow is over, they'll bring our stuff."

"Just try explaining that to a four-year-old—no tree, no decorations, no presents, and it's the first time he's been big enough to know what it all means."

I sighed, remembering how for weeks past, Johnny had chattered ceaselessly about the tree we'd have. Night after night, too, he crooned himself to sleep with a litany of its ornaments, always saving for last a huge silver-foil star — the Christmas Star that was to sparkle at the very top.

That's what hurt most, I thought, having to watch the youngster's certain disappointment, and with this storm now, there wasn't much chance to do a single thing about it either. Discouraged, I turned back to the window again.

At best, this bleakest, most remote lighthouse on either coast, perched as it was atop a hundred sheer feet of volcanic rock, was far short of being festive. Still. . . .

Here the *where* and *when* have created both problem and situation, so the story action is all in the present, and *fragmentary flashbacks* through dialogue and introspection will bring in any further explanatory material as it develops. This format is probably the one you'll use the most.

Character Opening using full flashback

If only Christie hadn't looked so — well, so forlorn as she trudged down the hospital corridor. If she hadn't, I might have managed to talk myself into really believing it was the best thing for all of us, including the baby we weren't going to have just yet.

Quickly I rubbed a hand across my eyes, and turned to the window. But staring out at a jumble of afternoon traffic I didn't even see the scurrying cars, instead it was the droop to Christie's slim shoulders, the way that cheap little red hat hugged her soft hair. . . .

Since this is a short-short confession, the problem is presented at once, then a full flashback concentrates on characterizing the young husband who feels that children must wait until he can provide them a really good home. His motive for pushing Christie into an unwanted abortion is right, but his values are wrong, and the change in him is brought about through an understanding of his own crippling. The "crutch" of those mistaken values dropped, he stands stronger — growing up to life.

While either of the two preferred formats could be used here, the story would spill over to a longer length, with a resultant slowing of pace that may risk interest. So, this is an example where the *full flashback* is a better choice. As I said, though, the material generally determines which of the three will work out to the story's advantage.

Narrative Opening (Chronological)

Honestly, I could hear Judy already. "What's everybody going to say — how'll I tell them at school!"

Now Ron, he was different. He wouldn't act like I was a freak, or as if I were doing something downright indecent.

"Gosh, Mom — gosh!" It's all my son would say, but I had eyes, didn't I? I'd see the flush of scarlet creep into his ears, catch the way his eyes avoided mine.

It wasn't going to be fun, I can tell you! After all, Joe and I'd been married eighteen years, and have two grand kids to show for it — Judy, almost thirteen, and Ron, a gangly seventeen. But here I was, expecting another baby at my age! Well, I've read plenty of stories and articles about this second family business, enough to give me a pretty fair idea of what was ahead. . . .

There's no need to go back any farther than today for motivating causes in this particular chronological story. The belated trailer to a half-grown family is enough motivation to an expectant mama who lets her children's likely reaction make a problem of that event. But suppose the narrator's blood type is RH-Negative, and she's afraid of miscarrying. If *Thou shalt not covet* was drummed into her as a child, and she has learned to suppress her feelings "because it's a sin to want things too much — something always happens," then you'll open with that love-hungry youngster, and move forward from there. And that will be your problem!

Dialogue Opening combining brief flashback and chronological

"Look, Gail —" Kim asked quietly, "why don't you and Jim just go and get married without all the fancy stuff — what's the use of it, anyhow?"

"But you can't do that," I was plain shocked at her denseness. "Besides, Dad isn't complaining about the expense."

I pushed down a nagging little concern about Dad. No, he wasn't complaining, but I couldn't help remembering the night I told him and Mom our plans. It was like I'd handed him a million dollars the way he acted.

"April is a fine month to get married, baby — the lilac bush will be in full bloom, and I'll rig up an altar right near the bay window —" then he smiled so darned sweet at Mom, "an altar exactly like the one we had in this very room."

Well, it didn't take Mom long to put a stop to any idea of a home-made wedding. She set her foot down, and set it hard.

"Every girl is entitled to have a really beautiful memory of her wedding —" she said firmly, and Dad sort of blinked his eyes hard, and turned away to polish his glasses. . . .

The characters are introduced and the situation presented here through dialogue, with a very *brief flashback* into the immediate past for motivation of the story's problem, as well as indicating the theme of every girl's right to a "really beautiful memory of her wedding." Then the action moves forward from there without further flashback. It's a good combination, avoiding disadvantages of both the chronological and full flashback treatments — I rather think you'll use it often.

There is also another type of opening I want to mention here, not because it's acceptable, but because it isn't! Verbalizing the theme as an opener is completely out of date, yet like those *purple flights* all writers dearly love, it still persists. Not in print, certainly, yet so many typescripts are submitted to me for criticism that start off with some nugget of wisdom, it seems advisable to include this example of the *philosophical opening.*

One of the saddest things in life is not taking the time to care enough. Oh, we care all right, and prove the depth of our caring in countless ways, but — well, there are too many "next times" that never become the here and now!

Maybe that's because time is something we all have, while money isn't. Whatever the reason though, most of us overlook just how much a few minutes can be worth because they don't cost anything.

There was Aunt Tottie, for instance. . . .

True Experience cut these first two paragraphs, and you'll see the result in Chapter 14 where the published version is our workshop mini-confession. When you *must* philosophize to get your story rolling, go ahead and do it. But do it only as a kind of primer, a superfluous appendage to be lopped off before submission.

Let's now look at that important other end of the story line — the real reason for a confession's being — the *ending.* The ending is what has given direction to every incident, every complication. It's where the narrator faces her problem squarely, and makes a decision that'll have a profound influence on her life, or life-style. And it brings into focus the theme, which is the characteristic plus of confessions, the "take-away" or lesson to be learned by readers.

Yet, for all its importance, the ending is probably the easiest part of your whole story to write. You've known all along — at least, I hope you have — what the resolution is to be, and the gradual change that's been taking place in your narrator's character now makes her climactic decision inevitable.

But — and this is essential — she must make that decision completely on her own. It must come from within herself, and be the result of definite action on her part. She can't just suddenly "come to realize," and she can't simply walk out of the mess, aided by advice somebody else offers. That's selling the readers short. To drag them through six or seven thousand words, then explain that there never really was a problem anyhow, will certainly bring on an editor's rejection.

Now, once the problem is resolved, you close swiftly — a brief paragraph to point up what the narrator has learned, the verbalizing of the theme. And then it's usually wise to add one more paragraph that gives a hint of her future course. You see, nothing ever really ends in life, except with death. So, because these are "true" stories, you should indicate a continuation beyond the story's end. Readers want some hint of how the narrator's decision will continue to have some effect on things she may do years later.

To show what I mean, here's the climax and ending of that shortie about abortion:

> I'd come farther than I realized, so to make it back before Christie was out of surgery, I hopped a cable car. And as it clanged over the crest of Powell, plunging precipitously to the bay below, I felt again the spurt of ice crystals on the cheek of a small boy belly-busting down snow-covered

slopes two thousands miles and a lifetime away.

Crazy, but my fingers touched wet when I instinctively wiped at their sting!

It was different then, I thought, getting off at the hospital stop. Living on a farm, and it wasn't such a dog-eat-dog world then either. Kids nowadays need a lot more though, don't they? That's why it was smarter to wait for our family until I could give them a decent chance.

Once this was all over, Christie would see it too, and — I pulled up short at the lobby door. Christie, she was sitting there, bolt upright and hat jammed uncompromisingly straight on her pale gilt hair!

"What the hell —" I broke off, the anger draining out of me.

Because I knew. I guess I always had, the same as Christie did right from the beginning. The same as Mom did those times she used to dig in her heels when Dad wanted to wait on things. Wait for next year's crop, wait until the mortgage was cut down some. Wait.

Wait — computerize life?

It was like dropping your crutch, and suddenly finding you'd never needed it anyhow. I didn't say anything, just reached to pick up Christie's overnight bag.

The talk would come later. But for now, it was enough to feel myself stand a little stronger — growing!

The "bones" of this ending are all here — the decision, theme, final wrap-up, and even the use of a symbol — and that's why I chose it, to make clear what goes into the confession's *take-away*.

However you handle it though, stay out of the pulpit! Nowadays editors all gag a bit at hand-wringing, God-forgive-me guilt. That has all been outgrown along with the old *sin, suffer, and repent* formula.

"A confession story properly ends in the narrator's strengthened maturity, or increased insight," Jane Bernstein, editor of *Intimate Story,* speaks for the entire market in pointing this out, "but let's have it fresh and real, written for Today."

Chapter Seven

Know Your Tools

If problem, theme and characterization are the bones of the confession, then the flesh and blood that makes the story hold up is the actual writing craftsmanship. You've got to master these structural techniques. While a full chapter might be devoted to each of these crafting tools, any good text on fiction goes into them in detail, so we're only going to look at their specialized application to confessions.

And don't flip through the next pages, doing what used to be called "piecing." Even though basic principles are the same, confessional technique is just enough different to require thoughtful study and practice.

Transitions

More than any other short story form, the confession relies on a continuity of action, the sense of motion that is inherent in life. Without this living breath of transition, your story will lack reality, and as a consequence, the essential *reader identification.*

But transitions can be a real hazard — if your narrator dawdles across a lengthy word-bridge going to work, the reader is bored; if she leaps the time lapse between shutting off her alarm clock and arriving at the office, the reader is confused. One tells too much, the other too little. So, unless something happens along the way that directly affects the problem, or is a foreshadowing of complications to come, a brief transitional sentence covers the change in place. For example:

> "Darn —" I opened one eye to glower at the alarm clock, reaching sleepily to shut off its jangle. *And I was still yawning when I got to the office* only minutes ahead of Miss Higgins. Maybe if I'd been more awake I might have seen how she. . . .

That spans a routine trip to work, and gets the reader set for the next scene. Or if your narrator is moving out of town, a single sentence will bridge the time it takes:

> By the end of the week we'd given away the fresh fruit and other stuff like that, and the rest of our things were already on the way to Phoenix.

And for a change of mood that might have supernatural overtones, the narrator is terrorized by eerie sounds during the night:

> Now there was a gust of wind that stirred the leaves outside, crackling them like brittle paper, then rushed down the chimney and swept the voice away.
>
> *Had there really been a voice?* In the sudden silence, I couldn't be sure. My nightgown clammy against me, I lay rigid, unable to move or cry out.
>
> Yet in the morning, with sun-fingers poking through the blinds and the house full of comfortable waking-up rustles, I almost convinced myself it had been just another of my nightmares. Almost!

The main thing is to carry your readers *with* you when traveling from-here-to-there, from-this-to-that, or from-now-to-then. And do it smoothly, without jolting them in he crossing of those bridges.

Flashback

While the transition implies forward movement, the technique for sorties into the past is similar, a word or phrase carrying the reader backward in time. You might compare this to the old Alley Oop comic strip that featured a time machine — your narrator steps into the time machine and by a transitional *had* or two, flashes back to an earlier period in her life, which then becomes the "now." In other words, once there, she tells her story as if it were currently happening.

Let's look at a full flashback first where the narrator re-lives events leading to the moment when she entered that "time machine." Suppose she's left her husband, and is newly arrived in Puerto Rico as a Peace Corps Volunteer...

>After awhile Mavis sighed gustily, "Why did you join, kiddo?" she asked. "What're you running away from?"
>
>*Running away — Ken had flung that accusation at me the night we kicked our marriage apart!* His fingers had bit into my shoulder, and he'd been so mad his voice shook, "You don't need guts to quit, Kati!"
>
>I couldn't tell Mavis how sick I'd gotten of trying to make too little money go too far, and how lonely it got with Ken moonlighting like he did. So I didn't answer her at all. I just squeezed my eyes shut against the picture of a lanky redhead who had zipped by my table that night four years ago...

But after they're married, frustrations mount up until Kati finally leaves him, and eventually winds up in the Peace Corps. That brings us up to the present again, and . . .

Now in the black velvet of a tropical night, all my tomorrows pressed in on me — what was I doing here? *Like Mavis had asked,* what was I running away from?

Do you see how easily "had" takes you into the flashback, and "now" brings you out of it? Cherish those two words, they'll stand you in good stead time and again.

There are times, too, when a flashback within a flashback will be useful, since it speeds the story action along by not having originally gone the whole way back. For example:

"Three kilos over—" the airline clerk slid my wardrobe case off the scale, and glanced at me as if he expected the usual argument about excess weight charges.

I just nodded dully and paid. After all, why shouldn't it be heavy? Why not, when inside lay a shimmery froth of satin, the virginal white untouched beneath folds of tissue? The suitcase held the fragments of a pitifully brief dream.

Less than a week ago I'd packed my wedding dress, my heart winging ahead across the Pacific where I was to meet Joe. . . .

The phrase *Less than a week ago* carries us into the first flashback, and the tragic death of Susan's fiancé just as she lands in Honolulu. After the funeral his friends insist that she stay on to get her bearings, but . . .

I'd never walked along the streets of Honolulu with Joe, never laughed, or kissed, or dreamed with him there.

Although they mean well, nobody seems able to grasp the importance of getting back to the Mainland before a single memory can dim, and . . .

Mr. Morgan was still arguing when he drove me out to the airport. "You have to go on living, Sue," he said. "Joe loved you, don't use his love to destroy the future! That's what—"

But I didn't want to hear any more of his advice. I told him goodbye quickly, and turned away to check in. All I wanted was to be alone— alone with my memories of Joe. . . .

Ordinarily, this would be our re-entry to the present, but we flashback again here, this time remembering the years when Susan was growing up to fall in love with Joe, and his return from a heavy construction job up in Alaska last spring.

It was then that Joe reached out his arms and, as if I'd been heading there all my life, I walked straight into them.

"Sue, honey — gosh, I was waiting for you to grow up, and here you've already done it!" he whispered, his lips closing over mine.

"Darling —" *for an instant I tasted the sweetness of our first kiss again,* then abruptly, the magic was lost in the confusion of take-off instructions over the plane's loudspeaker. . . .

Now, you're out of the second flashback, and have bridged the opening situation with no loss of pace in getting needed information across to readers. While this is somewhat tricky, there'll be times when it will come in handy to break up too heavy a load of background material.

Fragmentary flashbacks, the third of these time travelers, are perhaps the most useful. Woven into dialogue, or the narrator's thoughts, they're effective, yet not apparent.

"This isn't the way we came last summer, is it?" Beth fumbled for the road map, glancing over

at me a little puzzled. *"Golly, did I ever get seasick on all those curves!"*

That tells the reader the same trip has been taken before, along a different route, but it doesn't stop the forward movement, which is a technique often used in semi-chronological stories.

You will be using all three kinds of flashback — full, fragmentary and double — so work for facility in handling them.

Imagery

While imagery can make an acceptable confession an outstanding one, you must guard against "purple writing," those lush flights of fancy we all take off on at times. You may bleed a little at having to strike them out, but the "poignant cry of a lone whippoorwill," and the "flamboyant splashing of sunset's paint-pot," are not for the confession. Of course, you can use the loneliness of night-sounds, or the flaunting colors of a sunset to create mood and as a transitional device, but rely on simplicity of language, and an appeal to the five senses for their emotional impact.

For example, here's a bit of confessional imagery:

> There, in spite of myself, I felt the tug of the spreading purple haze on the horizon — the limitless stretch of the Pacific Ocean, and the whitecaps curling high in its closer waters.

Or this description of a logging campsite, and what a heat wave does in the forest:

> Well, like I was saying, it got so every bit of moisture dried out until even the evergreens had a dusted, thirsty look.

And a few words will paint a picture of the countryside:

> Plains with no limit, and broken mountains

reaching to the clouds.

The main thing to remember is that a touch of imagery can do a lot for any confession, but it must be kept in character — never, never let your narrator become "literary," or you'll lose the illusion of reality that's a must in this market.

Scenes

Don't duck scenes! Sure, it's easier to say,

> I took one look at Jim lurching in, and knew I'd had it right up to here. If he thinks more of the bottle than me, I told myself, he can have it. Because I certainly didn't have to put up with that sort of thing, and he'd just better believe it!
> Whirling, I raced upstairs and crammed everything helter-skelter into my suitcase. . . .

Action verbs keep that moving, but it's still as flat as yesterday's beer. Obviously, it's a pivotal point in the story, so why not let readers see this marital crisis actually happen? In other words, *show, don't tell!* When the narrator walks out on her alcoholic husband, the reader wants to live through that final break-up, too. But we're visually oriented nowadays, and unless she can see it all — recriminations, tears, door-slamming — the dramatic force is lost. Or, at least, weakened. So, always try to think in scenes, not narrative. And write them from the heart, because this is an important part of *confession tone*.

Don't, however, use scenes merely for their surface values of action and characterization. If you do, along with the narrator's "muddle," you'll have a "writer's clutter" to clear up!

Foreshadowing

Tipping the lid just enough to stir the reader's imagination and curiosity about what's to come, is necessary for suspenseful confession writing. It must not be obvious, and sometimes the mere turn of a phrase, or the seemingly casual remark of a character will do it.

> "I've got plans," Dale used to hint. "Punching a calculator isn't my idea of living — some day I'll latch onto a deal with real dough, then we can pull out of here and go places."

Any man stuck in a routine job could make such a remark, and it'd mean no more than the daydreaming we all indulge in. But when he happens to be the bookkeeper for an old-time investment company where customers often leave funds in trust together with their powers of attorney, you have a loophole for skullduggery, and that casual remark can *foreshadow* trouble ahead for the narrator who loves him.

> For no reason at all I shivered suddenly, like something had brushed the bright day, something dark and scary . . .

That may portend evil. But the same phrase, "something brushed the bright day," might also foreshadow tragedy, or perhaps a great disappointment, depending on how it's used in context:

> For a minute something brushed the bright day, something dark and sad. "Let's go out," I caught Bill's hand and pulled him toward the door. "It's too nice a morning to stay inside."

None of these three examples gives anything away, yet there's enough of a hint in each to alert the reader that everything isn't what it seems. You see, foreshadowing is like cooking with herbs, just a whisper is all that's needed. More can counteract the suspense it's meant to create.

Plants

Although the technique of planting is similar to foreshadowing, the purpose is different. When some dramatic development or character disclosure catches the reader by surprise, plants are the writer's answer to her amazed, "Well, for heaven's sake — how come?" Because all along the way, bits of stage business should have been "planted" which will point to this twist, and make it inevitable. But the trick is to weave in such *plants* so that readers aren't aware of them at the time, except perhaps as part of the immediate action.

If the narrator's conniving stepfather has murdered her mother, and manages to make it seem that she died as the result of an accidental fall down the cellar stairs, his guilt might be planted like this:

> Lunch wasn't cooking on the stove, but the kitchen floor was still damp in one or two spots from scrubbing, and the table was partly set. That meant Mom must be up by now, and rushing to get her work done before Sam came in to eat.
>
> Probably she'd gone out to the henhouse or to the barn for a minute, I decided, and began to rearrange the silverware, moving the spoons and knives to the right side where they belonged, and the forks over on the left. If I didn't know better I'd say Sam had been in and set the table, I thought absently, with him left-handed. . . .

The misplaced silverware and a just-scrubbed kitchen floor will both be remembered when murder is later exposed. As used here, of course, these two plants are what crime investigators term "physical evidence." But whether you're leading into murder, or infidelity, or any other significant happening, it can't just be dropped on readers without appropriate *planting*.

So, because plants are important to believability, look at your story objectively, making sure that the answer is there before some reader asks, "How come?"

Confession Language

Actually, there are no set rules for confession dialogue, only that you stay in character, and use common everyday words throughout. Your narrator is *telling* the story, remembering, confiding in an intimate friend. She is not writing a literary tome, or for publication, and doesn't express herself in formal language. Yet this is one of the things I've found confession tyros have the most trouble with. They persist in *writing* the story, parsing each sentence, avoiding participles that dangle, and making sure that every thought is completed. As a result, the necessary confessional tone founders in a Sargasso Sea of verbiage.

I'm not suggesting that you worry about such things in a first draft — get your preliminary thinking down on paper first. But when it comes to revising, if your narrator is one of today's teenagers, a Jesus Freak, a store clerk, a logger's wife, or whatever, then both narration and dialogue must be in the language this person would normally use. However, there is one exception — dialect and "in" expressions are better used sparingly. An occasional characteristic word or phrase gives the flavor, but a steady flow loses it. The reader too!

As for dialogue, each speaker is individual — and talks that way. The trick is to keep your dialogue natural, which means you'll break off midway in a thought, or suddenly switch to something entirely different, just as we all do in real-life conversation. Don't go on and on either — long, unbroken speeches are too formidable on the printed page, and deadly dull to read. Instead, suppose one of your characters is telling about a vacation trip:

"Why, you'll never believe the things Jim did getting ready for it," Bonnie sighed, remembering. "He started organizing things way back in March, setting up how many miles a day, and what to take, and —"

She said Jim made these lists of what was to be packed where in the camper, and when it was to be used, and checked each item off right down to the two strips of bacon apiece for their third morning's breakfast.

"I swear he even scheduled rest stops, and if the kids had to go in between — Hey, why didn't you say you're out of coffee?" she pushed back her chair, and padded over for the percolator. "But you know, we had a lot of fun anyhow —"

Here, *indirect speech* breaks up too solid a chunk of information, and preserving a sense of immediacy, also gives the impression of casual conversation. The same technique used in narrative portions creates the effect of *talking* a story:

Well, I'd tried, hadn't I — I wanted so terribly to make a go of it, but like Rod said, I was one hell of a wife. Couldn't even throw a decent meal together, and in bed — Oh, what's the use of going into all that. I wasn't able to hold Rod Lupo, so let's just skip it, hmm?

The mechanics of it, you see, are as much a part of confession language as the words. The main thing is to strive for the natural cadence of speech in dialogue, narrative, and stream of consciousness. Just talk, don't write!

There are many special tools we might go into, but as a confession writer, you'll be using those discussed here more than any other. So, if you learn to handle them well, your story will be easier to write — and easier to read.

Chapter Eight

The word is . . .

Aside from being first-person problem stories, what *really* makes a confession? Well, there's a word for it, but first let's take a close look at the eight elements every confession must have regardless of how problem and theme are handled, or who the narrator is:

Motivation

Things don't just happen, there's always a reason for everything. But without sound motivation, readers won't understand why your narrator acts as she does. And without this understanding, the very purpose of a confession is defeated. Because these are stories of human behavior, and the writer's job is to establish the cause of a narrator's character flaw, or mistaken attitude. With that clear, what she does in response to it is understandable, and engenders a compassionate concern for how she'll work out of the situation her own actions have brought about.

"How do I know what I'd do in the same spot?" the reader thinks. "Maybe if —"

To gain this kind of rapport though, you must have sympathetic motivation — spite, meanness, selfishness, or just plain stupidity, are too often used as the motivating force. And if you're tempted to do likewise, all I can say is — don't! Because, militant Libbers to the contrary, soundness of the home is still of paramount importance to the average confession reader. Food, for example, represents security to most of them.

Take my neighbor, she's not happy unless her cupboards are crammed to capacity, and can't wait to replace the can of corn or peas she opened for dinner. Silly? Not when she describes the sick panic of empty shelves and three small children to feed. That fear came out of the 1930's Depression, and now it's almost an obsession to never leave space unfilled in the canned goods cabinet.

Hers is an extreme case, of course, but it points up that the nourishment, safety and happiness of loved ones are universal needs even in our permissive society today. And a threat to any one of them is motivation for the narrator's immediate action.

This is where a working knowledge of behavioristic psychology is helpful because *what* she does depends on her character flaw, and the *why* and *how* of that must be shown to the reader's satisfaction. It's not enough for a high school "make-out" to justify her tabby cat ways by saying, "My folks didn't love me, so —" But if an elderly relative has taken that girl in from a sense of duty, and never lets her forget it, then you can develop the hunger for love building and building inside a lonely, confused youngster.

Maybe she'll tell how:

> Aunt Kate used to mutter that fruit never falls far from the tree. My stomach tied itself into a sick knot whenever she said that, because I knew she meant my folks, and the way Dad kept getting into scrapes while he and Mom were still living together.
>
> I was just past fourteen when they called it quits, and dumped me on Aunt Kate to raise. Everything that spells security to a kid had sud-

denly been yanked away from me, and I was confused and bewildered the afternoon she met me at the bus depot.

"Laurie, honey, I'm so glad —"

If only Aunt Kate had said that, and maybe cradled me close for a moment. She didn't though! Instead, she hustled me over to where the station wagon was parked.

"Fine goings on!" she snapped, her mouth a straight line. "I told your mother when she married him, Tom Barlow was a no-good. I warned her nothing but trouble would come of it, and I was right!"

"Please —" I tried to ward off the pelting blow of her words, "I won't be any bother, honest! I'll help you and Uncle Bill, and —"

"Course you will, Missy! I'll see to that, and I won't put up with any lally-gagging from you either. . . ."

A little more along this same line, and I think your heart would ache for that girl, even while you protested the substitute she finally finds for affection. So, here we can see that *what* the narrator does is the story, and *why* she does it makes the story happen.

Motivation is important to every phase of life, although under many different names. Take advertising, with sales the objective, motives are referred to as *appeal lures*. Similarly, the disease behind a symptom, the reason for a psychosis, the motive of a crime — each is the *cause* of an *effect,* or what the fiction writer identifies as *motivation*.

Sometimes it can be very slight, while other times the motivating force must be detailed and dramatically highlighted. But however much or little seems necessary to ensure the sympathetic support of readers, this element is vital to every confession story, because without it, characters and their reactions are not believable. You must, therefore, learn to use those two tools *why* and *what* effectively.

Identification

Actually, *reader identification* is an integral part of all confession elements, not a separate element in itself. The same problem may face many people, but as we've already noted, no two are exactly alike. So ask yourself, *What do I have in common with the ten million who read these flamboyantly jacketed magazines?* On the surface, perhaps nothing. However, the confession reflects life, and aims to illuminate it. And its writer shares with readers the universal experience of love and failure, and fear of the unknown — they see themselves mirrored in the persons living a particular story.

When they read about men and women in real situations, facing real problems as opposed to "hoked-up" fiction, they recognize their own problems, a neighbor's, or Cousin Susie's, reacting emotionally to every incident and situation. Birth and death, pre-marital relations, illness, divorce, delinquency — your life and mine.

And little things are the catalyst that makes my life yours!

If the narrator wraps yesterday's meat loaf in foil and, to take the curse off leftovers, pops a made-from-scratch chocolate cake in the oven too, the reader can relate to a woman who practices such familiar housewifely stratagems. Or perhaps the girl who works in a bank stays over to balance her cash, and is the last one out. . . .

> There'd been spatters of rain off and on all afternoon, but by the time I got through work it was sluicing down in a regular torrent. And me without boots, or even a head scarf.

We've all been caught like this, and know exactly how

she feels. But you don't just drop these aids to identification in here and there for effect — they're part of the action's forward movement, and should blend into it. . . .

 With my purse over my head for a make-shift umbrella, I darted across the street toward the bus stop, not even seeing the man who had just stepped off the opposite curb.
 "Watch it —" he put out a steadying hand, then I heard his breath suck in. "Lee — Lee Bradshaw!"
 Startled, I stared up at him in utter disbelief. "Steve, how —"
 "How did I find you?" he grinned, dark eyes teasing. "Nothing to it — I asked myself which of a couple of thousand towns in the fifty states you'd light in, and here I am!"
 "Steve Krakow — I mean really!"
 "Okay, I was down in L.A., and somebody said Bayview still goes for live music — what discotheque and folksingers have done to us trumpet men!" he tucked my hand under his arm, and before I could protest . . .

 Do you see what we've done here? We not only are beginning to identify with the narrator, but introduced a major character, and "planted" for what will be an off-beat problem, all within the framework of a situation that anyone can understand. And by continuing this technique throughout, when things come up that are outside the reader's own experience, she still is able to participate in them.

 You might say that *reader identification* is achieved through a kind of osmosis in going from the familiar to the unfamiliar. The confession, after all, is a vicarious happening, one that both writer and reader share emotionally with the narrator. When they do, the essential identification is there.

Reality

What makes for realism in the confession? An understanding of human nature, and the basic patterns of behavioral psychology is part of it. Authenticity of factual material is another, but only if it's presented in living scenes, not exposition. And know your market — give readers the sense of "it's happening to me," that the narrator's conflict with life is hers.

Such vicarious participation is what allows the "decent" housewife to see a prostitute's problem compassionately; the childless career girl to have empathy for a young wife with stair-step babies, and expecting another; the scrupulously honest to understand some one who is caught shoplifting and then tries to lie her way out of trouble.

But in striving for reality, don't make the mistake of thinking ten million confession readers want to hear all about the time your washer broke down in the middle of its spin cycle, and how you had to wring everything out by hand. Frankly, they couldn't care less!

On the other hand, there are times when a situation is explored in depth. Because the confession, besides being a self-help story, also serves as a source of information for readers. In fact, the documentary confession comes close to being a textbook, but presented non-technically while aiming to expand the readers' knowledge of certain subjects.

Take the mental health story as an example. It's not a narrator's understandable desire for release that's gone into, but the accumulation of detail describing what it is like to undergo shock treatment, to be imprisoned behind solid, double-locked doors, and no privacy for even the most intimate of body functions. Through her reactions to this experience, the reader gets a view of a world mercifully few of us are thrown into, and gains an understanding that can give comforting strength if mental illness strikes a member of the family.

Reality, you see, is a vital quality of the confession — its emphasis is a matter of judgment. Your judgment!

Action

Narration is used in the confession to cover time, link scenes together, and for introspection. But never to record action. That's a mistake writers new to the field often stumble over — they *tell* what happens, rather than letting readers *see* each crucial point of a story as it develops in live action.

However, even though that action is *a constant progression of the struggle element toward its conclusion,* it needn't be like the old Keystone Kop chase scenes. Sometimes only an involuntary gesture expresses greater action than a championship prize fight.

"Watch her hands —" a college drama professor once told our class when recommending that we see a certain stage play, "she says more with them than another actor does in a hundred lines — puts real dramatic action in just the way she lifts her hands or folds them."

Years later, writing about the piano player in a cheap Hollywood dance hall, I remembered that. He'd been headed for a career on the concert stage, but had injured his hand in Vietnam.

"Atrophied nerve, that's what the army medics called it — means I don't have full use of the fingers," Shep explained. "Oh, it's plenty good for the sort of thing I dish out at Dreamland, but that's about all now."

This accounts for his choice of jobs, but in a later scene with the narrator, when Shep talked about the dream he'd lost, it all sounded like "poor me," the carping of a beaten man. Yet, he had a right to be bitter, with his hand — and suddenly it was there, the *dramatic action* I'd been overlooking. "Watch his hands —" I told myself, as I began to type the scene again:

Shep didn't seem to hear, and it was as if he were talking to himself. "Before my folks died we had a little acreage near Petaluma," and he sounded almost reverent the way he said it. "Helping Pop plant stuff — the feel of soft, warm earth under my fingers — y'know, Kris, it was like a symphony!"

His dark eyes glowed momentarily, then his fingers clenched until the knuckles showed white and sharp, and he added under his breath, "An unfinished symphony!"

Whatever you're trying to get across, however, think of it in terms of scenes, not narrative, because that's how you get action into the confession story. And action you must have to sell in today's market.

Conflict

Conflict is another name for *opposition,* and when your narrator runs headlong into an apparently immoveable force, be sure it's a specific one. Something more than a vaguely hinted at, or fuzzy opposition. Ordinarily in confessions, this conflict is not physical, but mental or emotional. It can be gentle, or it can be completely shattering, just so long as there is a real block to the narrator and her determined course of action. Otherwise, scenes won't come alive.

So, the narrator must be well endowed with traits that either *make* or *invite* conflict. For example, an explosive temper makes for conflict with other people, and is almost certain to cause trouble eventually. Great ambition will too, and stubbornness, courage, idealism, intense fear, self-concern, deep love, greed, envy, conceit, even humility. Such traits should be selected carefully, or they can strain that "Golden Thread" of *reader identification,* but at least **one** strong *conflict-making* trait is important if a confession is to come off.

Weaker, although often quite useful for story purposes, is the *conflict-inviting* trait. The character trait that, under stress and strain of circumstances, invites trouble — a shyly innocent, inexperienced girl will go right on being safe so long as she remains in a protective environment. Thrown on her own in San Francisco's avant garde community, however, that innocence and inexperience will invite trouble. So, when it's out of character to give your narrator strong *conflict-making* traits, be very sure that she has *conflict-inviting* traits.

Then, too, you must be contrast-conscious. Like this:

> Beth was sitting on the sofa, feet primly together, hands in her lap, looking a little prissy and old-fashioned until you saw her eyes. They had that look I'd seen before, stony and challenging, relentless as a — well, relentless is all I can think of. And they were watching me.

Do you see what I mean? The sharp contrast between Beth's goody-good attitude, and that look in her eyes foreshadows something frightening to come. While very little is said here, just this bit of contrast is what creates a feeling of conflict.

There are countless ways to work in contrast — dialogue, personality, setting, emotion. However you do it, contrast highlights the point you're making, and strengthens reader-interest.

The contrast between *then* and *now* situations can also be used to pin-point the narrator's character flaw, or to sharpen the focus on theme. Take Kelsey. Fifteen years ago she kissed her soldier-husband good-bye after a week of marriage. "War is never good," Dave had said that last night together, "but without love to hold onto it's worse than hell!"

He stood looking down at our tight-locked fingers for what seemed an eternity, then his grip on my hand got even tighter. "Don't ever let go, honey — whatever happens."

I just raised our clasped hands to my cheek and whispered softly, "Good-bye, darling. I'm with you all the way!" And then I kissed him quickly, turning away so I needn't see the door close behind him. . . .

Now, he's been called back to active duty, and when this scene opens, Kelsey has flown down to say good-bye again. But she's determined to save her crying for later, and not let it spoil the little time left them. . . .

The instant I saw Dave I forgot all my good resolutions! He took one look at me, and knew — the welcoming glow faded from his face, and once more I had that feeling I'd failed him in some way. "Well, Kelsey," he kissed me lightly, "what shall we do today?"

"Anything — Dave, are you shipping out?"

"Yeah, tonight — let's skip it for now," he smiled at me thinly, and tucked my hand under his arm. "How about having one for the road?" . . . We had the drink in a small, dimly lit lounge. After awhile somebody dropped a coin in the juke box. Soft mood music began playing, and I choked up. "Dave —" I faltered, "Oh, darling — it's happened twice in my lifetime!"

At the same moment there was a sudden flash of light, and I looked up to see a brief-skirted girl smiling at us, her camera still aimed at Dave and me.

"The bars here all have photographers," Dave nodded to her, and said we'd take a print. When she brought it to us though, the picture mirrored our emotions too accurately — Dave tight-lipped, me with my eyes bitter and resentful. "Not much like the other time, is it?" he asked pointedly. "Well, it's a different war!" Suddenly I was shivering. ...

Without the emotional contrast of those two scenes, the narrator's conflict with herself might bog down to a dull preachiness. As it is, the reader senses that Kelsey has never really "let go" — that she's just gotten tangled in the string she's trying to tie onto tomorrow.

Don't go overboard about contrast though, and don't underestimate its power either in setting up the opposition to a narrator's attempts to cope with things.

The best tip I can give you for developing the necessary conflict is to make plentiful use of its special work words, *imagine, argue, act*. And keep the opposition real, specific, familiar, and constant — unabated trial and continued tribulation — within the confessional framework.

Lesson to be learned

Although structurally this element might be dropped and never missed, it is peculiarly characteristic of the genre and sets the confession apart from other short story forms. I suppose Aesop would've labelled such tagged-on endings *The Moral,* but that implies a *holier than thou* attitude, and readers tend to brace themselves against any preaching. Instead, the writer should think of the lesson to be learned as something a reader *takes away* to ponder upon later, perhaps finding needed comfort or guidance in it.

Take Kathy's confession, for example. Fifteen and pregnant, her soldier-lover disappeared into the limbo of overseas duty, she'd handed her baby over to "Mom" at birth, and assumed the role of a big sister. But as she matures, the ache of a denied motherhood sharpens, and planning marriage, Kathy flies north to claim her now twelve-year-old daughter openly.

How will Sharon react to their true relationship, she wonders? Oh sure, there'd be a temporary shock, but what about an adolescent's belief and trust in loved ones — might there be spiritual scars if her faith in the two persons she trusted implicitly were shaken?

They were waiting just beyond the barrier, Sharon fairly popping with excitement, and Mom — well, her face was wan and drawn, every worried moment since my phone call etched deeply into it. From the way she looked at me, eyes pleading and lips tightly pressed to keep them steady, I knew I had to relieve her anxiety as quickly as possible. But with Sharon hanging onto my arm, pelting questions about the trip, it was hard to see how to manage. I'd have to make a stab at it though!

"Honey —" I said as soon as I was able to squeeze a word in edgewise, "how'd you like to be a bridesmaid?"

Mom's breath sucked in sharply, and she put an arm around Sharon's shoulder as if to shield her from an expected blow.

"For you, Sis?" And in this, too, she turned instantly to share it with Mom. "Oh, golly, Mom, did you hear that — Sis got herself a fellow in San Francisco!"

I took a deep, hurting breath, and said it fast then, every word clear and distinct so Mom couldn't possibly misunderstand.

"And a big brother for you, honey!"

Across Sharon's head Mom's eyes met mine gratefully, with a compassion that told me I'd finally earned the right to motherhood, even though it must always remain our secret. This time I hadn't piled another wrong on top of the first ones! Oddly, it was like a benediction, bringing with it a sense of peace, and the realization that in keeping my daughter's tomorrows unspoiled, I'd also gained strength to endure the pain of sacrifice.

This is one version of the traditional treatment of the lesson, although there's also a more modernized form, in which it is not spelled out quite so obviously. So, let's try that final scene again, but with a little fuller lead-in, and a bit of pruning at its end:

> I'd tried to do what was best for my baby when I gave her to Mom twelve years ago, and it's all I wanted now too. Because no matter who she called "Mom," I was still her mother, and a girl that age needs a mother's love more than anything else.
> Did I love Sharon as a mother, that's what it came down to, wasn't it?
> They were waiting just beyond the barrier, Sharon fairly popping with excitement, and Mom. . . .

The rest of the scene is unchanged until Kathy relinquishes her daughter with:

> "And a big brother for you, honey!"
> I hugged my daughter close, and across her head my own mother's eyes were soft with tears. But proud too.

The same lesson — *two wrongs don't make a right,* and almost the same ending, except the second version's "takeaway" is now implicit in this one line of dialogue, and the brief concluding paragraph that underscores it. But keep in mind that whenever the take-away is offered swiftly as here, there must be a stronger preparatory lead into your wrap-up scene, or the lesson to be learned may not come through loud and clear, as it should.

As a general rule, though, I wouldn't use this treatment for the documentary confession, particularly those dealing with medical problems. You want to make doubly sure that readers understand the advice that's been passed along in fiction form, so a concluding summation is wise. As an example, take the story that discounts those Old Wives' tales about the RH-negative bogeyman:

> Of course, no two cases are ever exactly the same, but maybe mine can be a kind of safeguard against everything except your own doctor's advice. Listen to him, follow his instructions to the last letter — and go into labor unafraid!
>
> Some folks are bound to claim I've just been lucky to bear two healthy, normal children under the circumstances, and will insist we're plain foolish to risk the third one that's due any day now. Dr. Cranston, however, says with proper medical care, almost every RH-negative mother can be just as "lucky" as me!
>
> "Do you lock yourself indoors because there's a possible risk of getting hit by a car if you go across the street to the grocery?" he asked. "Why, every breath you draw, every step you take may be the fatal last one, Jennifer — so are you going to stop living entirely, and let your health, and spirit and emotions rot away simply because you're afraid to take a chance on the life God has given you?"
>
> Sure, there may be complications once in awhile, and sometimes a sad ending to the months

of waiting — that possibility is present in any pregnancy, whether it's an RH-negative one, or any other sort. We must be watched a bit more closely, that's all, and if anti-bodies do develop, there are ways to offset their danger nowadays. And that's why all of us RH-negatives should thank God for the very great blessing He's given us — the miracle of modern science!

But however a narrator tells of the lesson she's learned, the theme should also be neatly wrapped up in those concluding paragraphs and passed on to the reader. That aftermath, although anti-climactic, is still as essential today as it was when the first confession magazines came on the newsstands more than fifty years ago.

Emotion

What is *emotion?* It's what makes people feel alive, reacting to the world around them with their hearts, rather than intellect. Because we all live through our emotions — our response to religious ritual, the touch of a loved one's hand, the vicarious pain for a kitten's hurt, the "smell" of danger. Emotions.

And in the confession, emotion is not merely implied, but visible, audible and tangible. While the story's style is highly emotional, however, it's not purplish. The knuckle-white tightening of a man's fingers, or the smile on a woman's lips with bleak hunger in her eyes — these express emotion more fully than a thousand words of breast-beating and anguished *dear Gods*.

Actually, the confession writer should be an emotional sort of person herself to continue selling in this field over any great length of time. When I was in New York some years ago, Rose Wynn — an old-time and very fine confession editor — in discussing West Coast confessioneers, said that *action* came to mind when she thought of this one friend of mine, and *style* for another. Both qualities are important to confession writing, "But an editor will overlook a lot of mechanical faults if the writer has *natural emotion,*" Mrs. Wynn stressed, "and given that, we can work out the other with her as time goes along."

You see, emotion is something within the writer herself, and to come through in the confession, she must first feel it. Study how people FEEL. That's one thing we are all capable of understanding in others. We may not always be able to understand how they live, or accept their beliefs, who they pray to, or why they die, but we can all, with a little effort, understand how another feels.

This is the essence of what we mean by the emotional involvement of confession writing. You must know the narrator's emotions as your own — only then can you react as she would, and your readers share in that emotional reaction.

But don't underestimate your emotional capacities. I've only known two aspiring writers who had none at all. "I really don't like people," one of them told me, and that's probably the true reason they'll never be able to write a salable story. Certainly, they won't make it in confessions! Because to write confessions, you have to *care* what happens to a narrator, or readers won't either. And *liking* is a prerequisite to *caring*.

Watch this though — emotion must be continuing, not something that's dropped in here and there for effect. It's implicit in a character's reaction to conflict, and therefore, the result of characterization and motivation.

The important thing is, when the problem or material isn't sufficiently emotional to make it significant, the story is very likely to be rejected as "too slight." Remember, the confession must be an emotional experience for the reader.

Motivation, identification, reality, action, conflict, lesson, emotion — there you have them, the seven elements that are essential to every confession, no matter what its problem, theme, or format. Briefly, this is because:

Motivation makes problem and characters believable.
Identification is the sharing of another's experience.
Reality makes the unfamiliar familiar.
Action moves the story forward.
Conflict develops theme, and makes the story happen.
Lesson is what helps others help themselves.
Emotion — without it the smoothest written story is lifeless.

Yet, important as these are, one word says it all — *miracle*. Cliche, a word most of us use too often and too loosely? Not if you're a confession writer, because this word is the measure of every life you live — but only when it's spelled out thoughtfully and confessionally. M-I-R-A-C-L-E, before you put your story in the mail, always check it letter by letter:

M—otivation
I—dentification by reader
R—eality
A—ction
C—onflict
L—esson to be learned
E—motion

And now, let's add an "S" for the *sincerity* you must write with at all times — because honesty in your work is the cornerstone of a writer's professional ethics. I remember a woman who started in confessions the same time as I did, and how she used to deprecate such sub-literature, "We have to pretend to suffer even if we know it's all pretty corny," she'd shrug. "Poor dears, confessions are their only outlet!"

In her case, a smooth veneer on top of a cliche situation with none of herself in it, did sell three or four confession stories, because a facile style will rate an occasional acceptance — but, sadly, the well soon runs dry!

So, if you're unwilling to write yourself into every line, or feel embarrassed, or have to condescend — forget it!

But if you approach the confession sincerely, know how to use the basic tools of short fiction, and have mastered the unities of time, place and action, then there's a receptive market waiting for your submissions.

Chapter Nine

Better sure than sorry

It may come as a surprise to those who have yet to write a confession that research is important. Not the same sort done for an article, but research nevertheless, and it can't be shrugged off if you want to retain your status with confession editors as a reliable writer.

Personally, I don't like digging for facts. I'd much rather write with an eye to dramatic values, and my imagination free-swinging, yet each story I write sooner or later runs smack into points which must be confirmed or enlarged upon to carry it forward. Marriage and divorce laws, credit procedures, health problems, real estate practices, adoption requirements, regional terrain, occupational skills and jargon — you name it, and I've researched it.

It's a must — these first-person problem stories are read for much more than entertainment. Besides guidance, they also serve as sources of information, and since readers believe in their reality, the writer is obligated not to mislead them. So, if something is presented *as* a fact, you can't take factual license with it.

I remember the story a friend asked me to look over, a well-crafted documentary in which the narrator's little girl is hospitalized with a rare and baffling blood condition. I won't go into details, just that a young intern specializing in hematology has supposedly developed a serum that saves the dying child. So, I advised identifying the blood condition by its medical name, and more information about the newly discovered treatment.

"Do I have to name the disease — aren't technical terms awfully confusing to the lay reader?" my friend protested.

"Perhaps, but you can't drop a cure for the incurable on readers, then leave them dangling," I warned her. "Editors will want to know, and you might as well anticipate their questioning."

Backed into a corner, she "confessed" then that she'd made it all up, and incidentally, had done a very convincing job of it. She certainly fooled me!

"It made such a dramatic scene," my friend sighed, "and didn't really concern the story problem — are editors that fussy about fluffing stuff?"

Yes, Virginia — they are!

Editors have a right to expect absolute factual accuracy from their writers, just as readers expect it of the magazines. Besides, research isn't all that hard once you get going. Sometimes one question is enough. For example, while writing my story about the little bi-racial girl, I recalled vaguely hearing that blacks don't have a *moon* on their nails. A pivotal scene hinged on this, yet it was delicate to confirm. I went to the reference room of our public library for help with my problem.

"I've heard that too, but never gave it much thought," the librarian told me. "I'll tell you what, stand right here a moment — the stack girl is bringing up some books, and when she sets them down take a good look at her hands."

And that gave me the answer, because the "moon" on her well-cared-for nails was as clear as my own. While I did use that erroneous belief anyhow, its falsity was brought out later in the story.

Significantly, if I hadn't checked that one minor point, a lot of nice things would never have happened to me. One was that "Count Romance Out", my first published confession, drew more reader mail than any other *Modern Romances* story up to then. More importantly, of a "small sampling" the editor forwarded, nearly fifty letters were written by blacks, and none of them criticized my portrayal of racial characteristics, only the narrator's mistaken course.

"She should've known that you can't run away from yourself — didn't I see my own daughter try, and how nothing but grief came of it?"

That was the over-all reaction, and a couple in particular underscored *reader identification* by their heart-tugging comments.

"Thank God I read Jeannie's story in time —" one woman wrote, and the other ended her letter with, "God bless you, Jeannie — I pray for you every night!"

Remember those values of confession writing that I mentioned earlier? Well, to reach out your hand knowing someone, somewhere, may take strength from its clasp, is a plus that can't be pinned down to dollars and cents.

But suppose I hadn't asked that one question — see what I mean?

I can't tell you which or what in your story is going to require research, only that it must be done, and that the article writer's rule of *Answer before the reader asks* is sound advice for the confession writer too. Warning, though — don't do it so zealously your reader feels like the small boy who said, "This book told me more about penguins than I really wanted to know."

Following are the commoner areas that ordinarily require at least some research, even if it's only to get confirmation of your own knowledge.

Legal

Questions of law that are likely to come up most often relate to domestic problems — marriage, adoption, divorce and child custody. So, if you identify the state in which your story is laid, these will be some of the things to make certain of:

Is there a mandatory waiting period before marriage, and if it can be waived for emergency, what's the procedure? What is the statutory age for marriage without parental consent? Is a blood test necessary before issuance of the license? How about adjoining states, are the laws different there?

Who else besides an ordained minister may perform the ceremony? Are common-law marriages recognized; or when a young couple feels that love is the sacrament, not words and trappings, will their children be outside the pale of legal rights?

And divorce — what are its grounds, residence requirements and cost? How long does it take, and how soon afterward can one re-marry? What if the husband lets his alimony or child-support payments slide, can he be jailed for it?

A few minutes at the County Clerk's office should produce the answers to such questions. Or to go into one of them more deeply, you might talk to the Domestic Relations Judge (courts are usually located in the County-City building too). Marital problems are his job, and you'll find most public officials friendly and receptive to the serious free-lancer's queries.

Adoptions? There are adoptive agencies in every large city (check the yellow pages of your telephone directory), and again, the Domestic Relations court will provide needed information.

What happens if a person is arrested for shoplifting, or a hit-run accident? Or when there's been a rape, burglary, mugging? Is there a curfew for minors enforced, and how? Police can fill you in quickly, painlessly — and accurately.

There are several excellent paperbacks available, too, that briefly summarize the laws of individual states by subject, and are written in clear layman language. *The Legal Encyclopedia,* by Samuel G. Kling, *When You Need a Lawyer,* by Kenneth and Irene Donelson, and *Wive's Legal Rights,* by Richard T. Galen, are the three I keep handy for reference. However, because laws do change and confirmation is simple, I generally check with the above sources as well.

Of course, if you're lucky enough to have a lawyer in the family, or among your friends, be grateful — legal research is a snap then! But know exactly what you need beforehand so that your questions are brief and to the point. It'll pay off in cooperation both now and later.

Medical

Your family doctor is a prime source of information, but most physicians are too busy for chit-chat, and some take a dim view of writers besides. So, use your own judgment, and don't take advantage of his willingness to help. I have a well-thumbed copy of *The Popular Medical Encyclopedia,* by Dr. Morris Fishbein, and try to pin-point my problem first, organizing what I want to know in one-two order, and in *if-this-is-so, what-then-*fashion.

I had a particularly sticky bit of medical research once. I'd been doing stories on assignment from Bessie Little, and had heard of a man whose insurance company held off on paying his fire loss until the possibility of arson was investigated. Since excessive worry and emotional shock can create a mental stress that precipitates epileptic seizures, I got the idea of tying the two together. Mrs. Little liked my suggestion of a young couple's struggle with mounting bills, the miscarriage of an eagerly awaited baby plunging them still deeper into debt, and the harried husband's seeing a way out via their fire insurance policy while his wife is hospitalized. "But don't make it epilepsy," she wrote, "find something else that would have the same symptoms, etc."

Well, my doctor loaned me an armload of medical texts, and I set to work. You've heard of that *needle in the haystack?* That's what looking for "something else" than epilepsy between the covers of weighty medical tomes is like! Frustrated by multi-syllabled terminology, I finally gave up. This time Doctor Jim glanced along his bookshelf and handed me a slim volume by Dr. Alvarez, formerly of the Mayo Clinic.

"Maybe you'll find what you want here —" he shooed me on my way.

And I did! There in blessedly simple language was a discussion of *hysteria trauma* — causes, symptoms, prognosis. Among the various case histories outlined, was one that duplicated a form of epilepsy that is characterized by sudden rages and physical violence. Best of all, I now had an outstanding authority to back up my story premise.

Incidentally, to work out the arson angle, I contacted the Fire Department, and found out what they look for in such investigations, and our own fire insurance company filled me in on their end where arson is suspected.

You won't ordinarily get this involved though. A medical handbook on the order of Dr. Fishbein's, and a check of the *Readers Guide to Periodical Literature* at the library for recent layman-slanted articles should be all that's necessary.

I've lived through a good many traumatic experiences with my narrators — adjusting to diabetes, the miracles of eye and brain surgery, the onset of mental illness in a loved one, unfounded and founded fears of RH-Negative birth, blindness, cancer, the torture of perhaps bearing a drug-malformed child — and this I can promise you, the confidence with which such stories are sent off to market is more than worth the ordeal of medical research, whether it's major or merely routine.

Regional

A regional background is literally a plus to the confession. Incident and situation may grow out of it, but region should never dominate — the story itself must be capable of standing alone. The test is simple — if set in the middle of nowhere, would you still have a story?

Most regional research is looking into your own memory-bank. Suppose your home is in the Northwest. Timbered mountain slopes, the spray of surf on sandy beaches, and umbrellas lifted to December rains are old stuff to you — for someone out on the Great Plains, it's learning how the other fellow lives. So, for that person you'll work in the little things like weather and the rose you found blooming in the backyard on Christmas Day, or buying a cone of tiny coral-pink shrimp to eat on the way home from school. By bringing her into your narrator's daily life, she can identify more readily with the problem being presented.

Therefore, while traveling, the confession writer watches for these everyday, taken-for-granted things, and keeps notes for later reference when writing of a different locale than the familiar home area. Local customs, lay of the land, celebrations, odds and ends that add reality and verisimilitude. For more specific information as the need arises, the periodical room of your public library, travel magazines, and travel agents are excellent sources.

The Chamber of Commerce in any city is always cooperative, as are Triple-A offices, and the tourist information divisions of every state (the Secretary of State will route your query to the proper department). Letters to all of these, with a stamped return envelope enclosed, generally bring the specific material requested.

However, if you've always lived in some midwest prairie town, no amount of research is going to make your description of homesteading in Alaska seem real to the reader. Unless, of course, you know somebody who has lived there, and can draw a word-picture of it. For example, a friend of mine in describing the countryside around Juneau spoke with awe of the utter stillness. "It's so quiet, the silence shouts," she said. To a city girl, mightn't that complete lack of sound become unbearable? So, until I'm ready to write her story, this one-line description of Alaska's vast snow-muffled reaches is tucked away in the back of my mind.

That's what three-fourths of regional research amounts to — the writer's own perceptiveness. And a memory-bank to draw upon at will.

Occupation

Some occupations are strictly regional. A timber topper, for instance, won't be living in Florida's Everglades, and you aren't going to meet him in a St. Louis supermarket either. But any place along the Oregon or Washington coast, you'll run into high-climbers, their pants pegged and "corked" boots gouging the floors as they clump across. Service station operators, school teachers, waitresses can work at their jobs in Chicago, or Albuquerque, or Smallsville. So, you should always be sure that the occupation fits the locale. Then either from personal experience or contact with persons in that particular occupation, you do as in regional research, look for the ordinary little things to make it real.

Every occupation has a language of its own — doctors and nurses use the word *stat* to mean "on the double;" carnival workers speak of the *pitch* and the *nut* for the come-on talk that pulls a crowd into the show, and the necessary expense of putting it on; the radio disc jockey takes a "station break," and the stenographer a "coffee break."

In other words, a few commonly used phrases and typical duties are enough. You needn't turn your story into a job summary. Just normal observation will do it as a rule, and for the less familiar trades or lines of work, don't be afraid to ask questions of those engaged in them.

And once again, use the public library. You'll find *Career Novels* on the "Young Adult" shelves. These are written to acquaint a girl or boy with the requirements and preparation for almost any specialized adult field. Fashion model, nurse, physician, teacher, secretary, news reporter, beautician, social worker — the kind of life to expect for each is clearly depicted, and provides valuable source material for the confession writer, as well as built-in *reader identification*.

One occupation that is simple to research, yet difficult to handle, is farming. For some reason, writers find it hard to create the smell of hay, the atmosphere of a farm kitchen at daybreak, the scratching of chickens in the yard — the everyday life of an everyday farm. And yet almost any confession magazine will snatch up a well-written, plausible story with a farm background! The only advice I can offer here is to do first-hand research with your own five senses. Because if you try to get it out of books, or other secondary sources, you'll wind up with a scissors and paste job, which just won't get by in the confession.

So, don't think of familiar routines as dull, and don't leave out those little ordinary details that make your narrator's daily work come alive to persons who know little or nothing about it.

These are all mere kick-off points, and what or how much research you may have to do depends on the individual story. But in general, however minor, any factual material should be carefully checked out for authenticity. If it isn't, there'll be somebody to trip you, and that will earn you a nice big black mark in the editorial book!

However, if you're convinced that a certain thing is so, yet have trouble getting it confirmed, don't take the first authoritative word as the last.

Let me give you an example of this. When I visited a remote light station several years ago, the tower perched atop a 200-foot rock rising out of pounding waves, and lashed by gale-force arctic winds, fairly howled to be used in a story. A confession, naturally. The Chief Bos'n in command was manning it alone, because his crew of one had brought back a bottle of whiskey from shore leave. And liquor on the installation was strictly banned, so the seaman was relieved of duty.

Since the incident was one I wanted to use, I had to know whether it would call for a court martial, or what? But the Coast Guard officer I talked to on the telephone informed me the situation simply couldn't happen.

"Suppose it did, though?" I persisted.

Impossible. It was against regulations, ma'am!

The public library settled the issue. Thirty minutes with a set of Coast Guard regulations gave me the answer. Not a formal court martial, but a *Captain's Chair* is held under such circumstances. The penalty? Loss of rating, and time in the brig.

You see, sometimes the very person who *can* provide the necessary information, *won't*. What motivates that refusal is unimportant here. I can't tell you when to take "no" for an answer, and start dreaming up a substitute. That's up to your own judgment and instincts. But if you feel your "authority" is deliberately holding back, use your own ingenuity to dig out the needed fact elsewhere.

If you're wrong, a little wasted time isn't going to cost more than a momentary irritation. On the other hand, if you're right, that one bit of research could be the difference between a sale and a reject.

So, learn to rely on research. You won't use all the material gathered, of course, but it does enter into your writing and gives an identification that comes through to the reader. More, with proper research, you aren't guessing or glossing over facts — and it's a comfortable feeling to know that if anyone challenges some point, you can quote book and verse for your source.

Chapter Ten

What Happens at Your Typewriter

Every story is unique, and depending upon your personal view of the problem, its development is too. As I've already pointed out, no two of us react exactly the same to any given situation. Our background, nature, weaknesses and virtues dictate thought as well as action, literally grinding the lens through which we see the world. So it follows that you may focus on one facet of a story germ, while I may look at another which leaves you completely and inspirationally cold.

I remember when the body of a young beauty school student, raped and beaten to death, was found some years ago in an isolated part of a park. No clues, except that the girl and one of her classmates had been absent the day before, and that the elderly caretaker who discovered the murder victim was rather an eccentric. Not much for police to go on, but to three of my confession-writing friends there were story-clues all over the place.

One used the park attendant to build up a circumstantial case against him as a sex-crazed loner, entangling the crusty oldster in a web of unfounded gossip and mass hysteria. Another was stirred by the anguished parents' self-blame, and the might-have-beens that almost destroyed them. And the third was intrigued by the victim's unexplained skip from her beauty classes. She used the "what if" method, and dreamed up a real shocker about the two girls having cut school to go out with a pair of soldiers stationed at the nearby army camp, boys they'd met earlier at a U.S.O. dance, and had been secretly romancing since.

Two of these stories were bought by the same confession editor, so you can see how unlike they had to be, yet both were created from the same situation. But the truly amazing sequel to the last story sketched above, is that nearly ten years afterward, the survivor of this stolen holiday went to police with an eyewitness account of the murder, pinning the crime squarely on one of the servicemen who had become enraged when he couldn't make it with her friend. She'd been kept in terror ever since, first by post-hypnotic suggestion, then by his long-distance threats to "get her" too if the truth was revealed.

When somebody says flatly that certain material allows no choice of narrator, or is only suitable for a particular type of story, I hope you'll think back to this "true story" and take such expertise with a grain of salt. The focus is all in the eye of the beholder.

Similarly, most problems will fit into any one of the four major confession categories. Take alcoholism, as an example. You, as narrator-writer, will decide which exemplifies your chosen theme best . . .

The breakdown of homelife, whether it involves the frustrations of an alcoholic's wife, or the effect upon a sensitive adolescent, offer endless possibilities for the *Family Problem* confession, and would probably be more effective told from their viewpoint than his.

If you want to put the emphasis on symptoms and treatment of alcoholism, then the *Documentary* is your best bet, particularly if you've gotten onto some new medical or psychiatric theories and treatments to serve as your vehicle, and provide hope-giving information on what seems a hopeless problem. This type of confession might have fuller coverage if the alcoholic is narrator, although again, a close family member may work out better. That's up to you. Incidentally, youthful drug users are a serious problem today, but what about the teenage alcoholic? This is also causing considerable concern, but in story form, it's still pretty much virgin territory, and worth exploring.

Then the *Inspirational* confession. I know a retired army officer whose fight to cope with alcoholism fits all four corners of that category. Change him to the young G.I. back from active combat duty, but the tensions of it still with him, and you could do a poignant, inspiring story of *God up in Heaven, Hell down below, and in between earth as the stage for the show.*

And finally, there's the *Tabloid,* or behind-the-news yarn. The horror of crime committed in an alcoholic "black-out" is just one of many sensational confessions which can be developed here.

Actually, the majority — not all, but most — of confession problems are capable of being handled within each of these categories. You, your theme, and available material determines which it'll be. So, first live with the idea that has sparked your imagination until an awareness of its meaning emerges, and what message you want to convey by it. This preliminary exercise is writing, too, and will save a lot of false starts. Once you have the theme and the shape of a story in mind, your own work habits direct what happens at your typewriter. Every writer goes about a story differently. Some chart its actual course beforehand.

I like to take a firm grip on the "golden thread" of *reader identification,* and write straight through from beginning to end, getting my entire story down on paper as quickly as possible. Normally, I do three drafts, this first rough one, its revision, and a smoothed, polished version. Yet, I have a friend, whose many short-shorts have appeared both with and without byline, who goes at it quite differently. She does the first draft in her own mind, perhaps while ironing or washing dinner dishes. When she's mentally polished each word until it sparkles, she dictates the story to herself on the typewriter, and that's the final draft.

Still other writers work paragraph by paragraph, drafting, revising and polishing as they go along. And when the end is reached, the story is ready for submission.

Now, suppose an idea hits you. Explore its meaning for yourself first, then think about what meaning it might have for others. When those two sides of the idea meet, yours and the reader's, the story will begin to emerge. Before we go any further, however, let's make it crystal clear that the confession is not a gaggle of separate parts to be manipulated into a whole.

When you get an idea for a story, you should also get some inkling of the form it will eventually take. But you don't just write the basic story, then lard in the emotion. Instead, you heighten by incident and conflict the emotion that's merely implied in your first draft. With it down on paper though, you might take three lines of straight narration, and through scenes, expand them to three double-spaced pages of *emotional action*.

And this isn't "larding in," it's *developing* what's already there, but written in literary shorthand. See the difference?

So, learn to *think* of your story as a whole, right from the start. Visualize it as a lump of modelling clay, flexible and reworkable at any moment. But it's impossible to *talk* about several things all at the same time, and if I tried, I'd end up confusing both you and myself. For purposes of simplification, therefore, I'll do it as though the writing of a confession is divided into separate stages.

The order of these is not important. In fact, piecing together a story is somewhat like making a dress. The material and pattern are selected, but maybe you're long-waisted, or have size 12 hips and a 14 bust. You allow for this variance in the cutting, and when it comes to the sewing, darts, and easing and tapered seam allowances fit the dress to your figure. And it doesn't matter whether you've put in the zipper before the sleeves, or seamed the skirt first and then the blouse. The final effect will be the same either way. The important thing is, dress or confession, that basic procedures are observed in making it individually yours.

Okay? Then let's take a look at the necessary elements of a confession, which we'll call the *Five Stages.*

Stage One — Narrator faces a problem.

You open with a scene that sets the stage for the "muddle" ahead. Dialogue, or live action probably hooks more readers than straight narration, although a definitive statement can be effective too. But the once popular philosophical opening — *When you stop to think, it's true what they say about the longest journey starting with just a single step, and that goes for whether it's around the world, or into heartbreak* — should be left where it fell from grace in the mid 60's!

However you get into the story, though, the narrator's immediate problem requires that some decision be made, and it in turn triggers the action, the result of which will have a lasting influence on her life. Even if your chosen problem is seemingly trivial, it sets the action in motion since the narrator has a besetting sin — a *character flaw* — that is either the reason she's faced with such a problem, or motivates her attempt to cope with it in the way she does. Whatever the *flaw* — envy, or stubbornness, or a hungering need to be loved — it's an integral factor in your story's development, and as necessary as *theme.*

So, for Stage One, confront your narrator with the problem she must solve. Create an incident that brings it into sharp focus. And make her decide to take action. As an example, take the idea of *hysteria trauma* that I discussed in our chapter on research. The problem, you remember, was the husband's incipient breakdown, a symptom of which is his hang-up that the narrator herself is mentally sick. Here's how I opened that story:

> "I phoned Doc Schultz this morning, Marge," Kevin said, swinging around from the sink, reaching for a towel off the stack I'd just folded.
>
> "Wait —" and I tried to steady them before the whole bunch tipped onto the kitchen floor. "I'll get it for you, darling."
>
> But Kevin was in one of his moods, and it was almost as if he wanted to make me fly off the handle the way he jerked the towel free, then kicked the tumbled mass of fresh laundry aside.
>
> "Don't be so jumpy," he shouted. "a guy even tries to tell you something, and you carry on like a — yeah, it's a damn good thing I got sick of your shilly-shallying, and made an appointment!"
>
> I knew from his tone there wasn't a bit of use arguing this time. What's more, I knew exactly why he was bound I'd see the doctor — my husband thought I was going crazy!

Here, I've tried to make the reader wonder, "What is Marge going to do — what if I were in her spot?"

Stage Two — Background leading to problem.

This is where you motivate your narrator's actions — an absolute must in every confession. It's done by flashback, but now the chronological story is favored, which means you'll bring in the motivation by fragmentary flashbacks. Of course, some confession problems still are better adapted to the old full flashback. In those cases, go back however far you must in order to establish the cause of the narrator's *character flaw,* but don't stay in the past any longer than necessary. Instead, be selective about the incidents that have shaped her character, develop them clearly, and get on with your story.

The important thing is, there must be a completely acceptable reason the narrator is dominated by this fateful *character flaw.* Or in a nutshell, *the cause is a logical motivation of the effect.* Otherwise, your narrator isn't going to be sympathetic, and that's another kind of *flaw* in the confession field, one that results in rejects.

So, now we have the narrator faced with a problem, and moved by a character flaw that's been soundly motivated. Let's go on to . . .

Stage Three — Narrator attempts to solve the problem confronting her.

Although your narrator has a choice of action, she acts impulsively from the heart, and because of her character defect, it'll be the wrong decision. This will lead into the "muddle" and the necessity for other decisions — all wrong. But if you've kept the narrator sympathetic, and motivated each new development through *cause* and *effect,* the reader won't condemn her for those mistaken twists or turns. She'll anticipate the consequences, and worry about the outcome, identifying herself or someone she knows with the narrator's effort to work things out.

Stage Four — Results of narrator's attempt to solve the problem.

Here everything peaks. It's the inevitable outcome of all that has gone before, and is an apparently hopeless situation for the narrator. It's the climax.

If she's been making the drug scene, she'll perhaps freak out; if she's lied to alibi her husband, she'll be trapped herself; if she's taken advantage of the liberalized abortion laws, she'll find that it has made her sterile . . .

And she sees now that the fault is all hers, and recognizing her *character flaw* for what it is, wants to do everything possible to set things right again.

A word of warning though. The narrator can't just "suddenly realize" what's been wrong all along. The signs have been there, but she hasn't stopped to read them, or tried to understand their meaning before. Now, she stops rushing blindly ahead, and really looks at things. It's her problem, nobody else's, so she can't walk out of the whole muddle aided by a convenient crutch you hand her on page 20 or 25!

Stage Five — Conclusion.

If you possibly can, without having to contrive it, make the ending happy. Give the narrator a second chance, or a ray of hope at least. After all, the character defect that's been at the bottom of it all, is one many of us may have — "There but for the grace of God —" the reader should be able to say.

But don't just tag on this wrap-up. Have a scene in which the narrator indicates by her *actions* that she wants to make restitution, even though she expects nothing for herself. Then, through that attempt to undo her wrong, she may find the second chance at happiness.

But remember, while this is a basic pattern for the confession, you'll be taking darts in it, or letting out the seams to fit each story you write. The modern girl who believes it is more honest to live with her lover openly doesn't react or see things in the same light as the girl who holds marriage as the sacrament of love. To one, without the ceremony, a sexual relationship is a shameful tarnish. To the other, it's having the courage of her convictions. Either premise can be used in today's confession story if you work with people, not situations, and adjust the pattern to fit the individual narrator.

In the two chapters that follow we'll look at how it's done. I've taken one of my own published stories as an example of this genesis of a confession idea.

By following my story's development, you can see the actual conception of a confession, its gestation and birth. And this analogy of being "with Confession" is just that. The confession writer literally feels, or should, the growth within from embryo to delivery.

Perhaps we're more emotionally involved than our writing peers, but producing a confession really isn't much different than having a baby! I know that I'm drained at the end of each one, yet there's always a sense of fulfillment I've never experienced in any of my other writing.

So, turn the page to learn why and how this one woman faced a shattering crisis in her life.

Chapter Eleven

Genesis of a Confession

My idea for the story that follows came in two parts, with nearly three years between. A friend had received a whiplash in an automobile accident while on a business trip, and before he'd fully recovered, suffered a stroke that garbled his speech and left him partially paralyzed.

That created the back drop for the first half of this idea, although I didn't think of it as story material until much later. But paging through the newspaper one evening, I ran across a syndicated medical column and my interest was caught by a statement that *the family of a stroke victim is often more in need of care than the patient himself.* The lack of communication, it said, and stroke-induced personality changes can create pressures that are emotionally too much for them to handle.

What if I wondered, immediately thinking of Bill and Mary, and how hard it was to carry on a simple conversation with him, even after three years of therapy. What if it had been *my* husband who'd had that stroke? Would I be able to take the strain of an extended convalescence without something giving way?

It seemed an ideal problem for a confession, although I'd have to know more about the medical side before letting my imagination take over. In this instance, the *Reader's*

Guide to Periodical Literature put me onto most of what I needed on cardiovascular accident, including case histories of the "personality changes" that can make an easy-going man a family tyrant, detailed discussions of treatment to help restore mobility to crippled limbs, and how speech therapy channels new brain patterns where the old have been destroyed by stroke. One article mentioned something that really intrigued me — Grandma who has never said a thing stronger than "drat" in her life, will often spew out words which would stop a skid-row bum in his tracks.

But I wanted to use the wife as narrator, and none of it made her come alive. So I started another story, letting the stroke idea rest awhile longer. It kept nagging at me though.

While I had a working model in my real-life stroke family, they were in their early 40's, and today's confession reader prefers young marrieds, under thirty if possible. However, my doctor reassured me that a CVA can occur at any age, and even small babies have been stricken. Then he tossed in that impotency is sometimes a complicating side-effect — and I had it!

You see, I'd been thinking of stroke as my *story problem* instead of the *motivation* for it. Sure, I thought, the husband's impotency could lead to adultery. And the narrator needn't be a sex-pot either, just an ordinary wife trying to cope with a suddenly extraordinary life.

Until then, too, I was groping for the *character flaw* to catapult my narrator into adultery, but everything that might serve seemed contrived and out of character for the kind of wife I felt this girl should be. While confession stories demand such a defect, and I'd have to come up with one sooner or later, the stroke situation and resultant problem could happen without her having any flaw at all.

With that momentarily disposed of, there was only *theme* and the problem's *resolution* still to pin down before starting to rough out a first draft by my favorite method of *what if* and *suppose.* Since my real purpose in writing this story was to get information on strokes across to readers, *To know is to understand* seemed a ready-made theme. But I also wanted to end on an upbeat, and to do that I felt the husband must discover his wife's adultery, yet be understanding of its having happened. This gave me the theme *To love is to understand,* which the resolution would exemplify, and at the same time, offer the desired *ray of hope.*

The actual incident precipitating the adultery would come to me as the story progressed, but now I knew where I was headed, and that my narrator's marital transgression was the result of her being an ESV (*emotional shock victim*), which tied in with the basic premise of a stroke patient's family often needing more care than he does himself.

So I was ready to start, using questions and answers — cause and effect — to build my story. This point in confession writing could be called a crossroad, because you can take one route or the other, and still reach the same end. The method-writer will plot, incident by incident, knowing in advance exactly what the narrator must face and how she'll respond to every complication.

Fine, but human nature is unpredictable, and when you set the stage beforehand, then tell your narrator, "Alright, Susie, there's your cue, now go ahead and commit adultery," she may balk at violating her marriage vows. And only considerable contriving on your part will force her performance. Myself, I've found that climbing inside my narrator and doing what comes naturally to her is the most viable, and it's how I went about "living" the story of a young wife, and what happened "Because He Couldn't Be a Real Husband," the cover-featured title *Modern Romances* gave it.

But — and there always is a "but" where characterizations are concerned — she'd have to be entirely sympathetic throughout, or my theme was an empty premise, without the necessary help for others. And even though confession readers are coming to accept pre-marital sex, adultery is something else again, and it was going to take a lot more than sex-frustrations for the reader to say, "I don't know, maybe I'd do the same in her place —"

How could I justify it though, what would make that unknown reader understand?

Suppose the wife goes back to work to build up their "baby fund," I questioned, and what if the husband gets a promotion that means moving to another town several hundred miles distant? Won't she hesitate to quit her job until they're sure his is okay? The expense of a possible double move alone calls for caution, doesn't it?

Well, let the husband go on ahead, commuting weekends. Then his car accident and the later stroke as it happened to my friends . . .

Slowly, the story evolved in my mind — therapy sessions, the husband's futile attempts to make love, the horror of what his sexual failure does to him, and the long-time friend who stands by them through it all.

What if something jerks even that strength away from her — suppose this happens? Each answer was leading me closer to the story's problem, adultery — and what then?

No, I wasn't plotting, I was acting and reacting as this one particular woman would. There were many times when I'd think she should do a certain thing to move the story forward, yet Peggy had a way of stepping down from my typewriter carriage and going ahead on her own.

This is one of the advantages of building a story through characterization. Your main characters aren't just acting out the script handed them. They're real human beings actually re-living a crisis in their lives, and because they are, the important sense of *reality* comes through. I remember hearing Irving Stone say that the writer of biographical novels must be three persons all at once — the reader, the writer, and the one whose life it is. And that's true of confession writers, too. Yours is the heart that tells, the heart that records, and the heart that listens.

I'm not going to detail the specific incidents and complications that my *what ifs* developed, and I'm not going to go into how I drew on personal observations and philosophies to give the plush of living to this bewildered young wife's experience, it's all in our workshop story, and I'd rather you read it first like any non-writing reader would, without the influence of a preconceived pattern.

I've selected "Because He Couldn't Be a Real Husband" for analysis since semi-documentaries are pretty much timeless, and with strokes common to people of all ages and economic levels, the basic documentation has universality. Then, too, it's also a human behavior story, and all the required confessional elements are present, so the genesis of this one woman's confession from idea to printed page will point the way to putting together almost any other first-person problem story.

I want you to read through the following story as a whole, which is how it was written. Marginal notes identify the five stages of structure, the component elements represented by our Miracle Word, necessary research material, and invention. Study these on your *second* time through, and only then, read my brief wrap-up summary that explains why I decided on the format used and the scenes to be dramatized. I think you'll find this and the explanatory annotations can be fitted to your own thought processes in developing a confession idea.

Now, we'll let Peggy tell about her husband's stroke and what it did to their marriage . . .

Chapter Twelve

Workshop

"Because He Couldn't Be a Real Husband"

Reprinted by permission of Dell Publishing Co., Inc., from
Modern Romances

1 It was a wonderful party. Dejays, newscasters, technicians, just everybody from KMPC came at one time or another, filling our little three-room apartment to bursting, and the way they dived into the food, you'd think eating was going out of style tomorrow.	1 thru 10: Sets scene; introduces main characters. Stage One.
2 As always, Dave kept things humming at top speed. That husband of mine had twice as much energy as any one man needs. But I thought he looked tired beneath his exuberant gaiety — and no wonder. If he'd slept more than five or six hours since getting up on Friday — and this was Sunday — I don't know when he managed it.	2 and 3: Plant (Dave's overtiredness from commuting, and its result — Par. 14)

3   "With a 200-mile drive still ahead of him too!" I sighed to Tuck — Lester Tucker, he's station manager here, but Tuck is also Dave's best friend since way back when, and the guy who got him this chance to take over the new Manning outlet. "Do you radio men all have some kind of a secret formula?"

4   "Dave is just one of these human dynamos, and doesn't need sleep to re-charge

102   *The Confession Writer's Handbook*

himself," he shook his head ruefully. "I do though — swell party, and give me a ring if you need anything during the week, Peggy."

5   And it really was a *swell party*, although I was relieved when it finally broke up a little after two in the morning. Once the door had closed behind the last straggler, I stood on tiptoe to kiss Dave, then simply collapsed on the sofa.

6   "Tired, sweetie?" he patted my cheek understandingly. "Look, let's plug in the percolator for a quick cup, and I'll get you tucked into bed before I take off — okay?"

7   "I wish you'd wait for morning —"

8   "Not a chance, Peg — I've got a network show to monitor at eight, and our jalopy isn't jet-propelled!"

9: Foreshadows problem. Theme.

9   He scooped me into his arms, and as it had been so many times in the past, I was awed at the way our bodies responded to the slightest touch of the other's. Like talking with all our senses, instead of words. Dave used to claim if you can't do that, there isn't any true marriage either. Just a shell, a kind of false front to fool outsiders, and empty inside.

10: Transition — time bridge.

10   Anyhow, I was asleep when Dave slipped out of bed that Sunday night, or rather Monday morning, and the phone had probably rung ages before its jangle penetrated to me.

10 thru 27: Incident that leads into problem. Scene here has all component elements of

11   Bet it's a wrong number, I thought, stumbling barefoot out to the hall. Sure, and they'd hang up the minute I got there!

12   "Mrs. Eagan — Mrs. David Eagan?"

13   Suddenly I was wide awake, my mouth dry, and tongue incapable of sound — Dave was hurt!
14   "We think he may have dozed at the wheel, Mrs. Eagan," the disembodied voice went on and on. Something about Dave running off the road. Something about the State Police finding him unconscious.
15   Something about a hospital. Somewhere.
16   "He's dead, isn't he — Dave is dead, and you don't want to say so!"
17   The receiver dropped from my hand, banging against the table. An eternity later, the crackling sound stopped.
18   Now there was nothing but the silence. And fear!
19   Who had called me — where was Dave? I snatched the dangling receiver, and pressed it to my ear. Nothing. Not even a dial tone!
20   Frantic, I jiggled the phone, screaming at the operator to ring for me. To find Dave!
21   "Sorry, madam — I must have the party's name, or number," she said, maddeningly officious.
22   "It's Tuck —" I sobbed hysterically, snatching at the only name I could grab hold of. "He's at the station — please, I need him!"
23   Thank the good Lord for operators with imagination, and the ingenuity to pull a flesh and blood man out of that! I don't know how she did it, but I was still standing

Miracle Word, except the letter "L," Lesson to be learned.

22 thru 32: Preparation for narrator's dependence on Tuck.

there, the phone practically frozen to my fingers, when Tuck opened the door with the janitor's passkey.

24   What's more, he had already contacted the State Highway Police and found that Dave had been taken to the Altamont hospital, a few miles this side of Manning.

<small>25 thru 27: First half of story "germ" (See Chap. 11, Genesis).</small>

25   "Nothing serious, Peggy —" he reassured me. "No broken bones, or internal injuries, just a possible whiplash, and a knock on the back of his head."

26   "How, Tuck — what happened?"

<small>27: Plant for narrator's character flaw.</small>

27   He shrugged. "The Doc says Dave isn't even sure himself — thinks maybe he dozed off for a minute and missed the curve."

28   Tuck drove me straight to Altamont, and they let me see Dave at once. Frankly, I thought he looked awful, white as a sheet, and his head held immovable by sandbags at each side.

29   "My favorite nurse!" he grinned weakly, his eyes closing again.

30   "Heavily sedated — probably won't wake up for hours," a nurse rustled in, reaching for Dave's wrist, and jotting a notation on his chart before she re-hooked it at the foot of the bed.

31   She smiled then, and told us there was coffee in the staff room, or if I wanted to rest awhile, she'd show me to the Nurses Lounge.

32   Later, after Tuck had talked to the doctor and they'd pieced together what little **information there was,** he drove on to Manning to arrange for someone to fill in, tem-

porarily, at the radio station — the station where Dave had just taken over his wonderful new job of manager.

33 It was only then that I remembered to call my supervisor at the hospital where I worked as a practical nurse, explaining why I hadn't come in this morning.

34 "Don't worry about a thing, child," she was all sympathy. "Stay right there with your husband — when you're ready, just give me a call."

35 Which was a relief. That I'd still have a job, I mean, in case Dave was laid up any length of time. Strange — and terrible, too — how important that job of mine kept being. "It's only until we get enough in our Baby Fund," I promised when Dave howled about a split-shift marriage, him doing KMPC's Night Owl Show, and me on days at St. Joseph's. And he was willing to go along with that for awhile anyhow.

36 Then three weeks ago, they made Dave manager of KTW, the chain's new outlet for eastern Oregon, and he thought I should quit on the spot. But suppose it didn't work out for us in the new deal, and we had to come back here again?

37 "The way they charge for moving just across the street — Dave, it's almost 200 miles to Manning!" I fretted. "We ought to be sure first."

38 "No problem, honey — we can stay at a motel to begin with, and not bother moving our stuff for a few weeks."

39 Except that meant paying double

35: Flashback that helps explain Peggy's job. Foreshadows action and conflict that is its result.

36 thru 39: Peggy's character flaw of being too practical, and her tendency to "cross bridges."

36 thru 52: Stage Two. Sets up situation which is first link in chain of causes for problem.

rent and Dave's raise wasn't effective until the next month — I don't know, the more we talked, the more complicated the move became.

40: Wrong decision, motivated by narrator's character flaw.

40   So, we finally decided Dave would take a room in Manning, and I'd hold my job until his had shaped up. Being separated like that wasn't forever, and the extra I'd be earning could take care of the moving expense. Besides, I told Dave, we'd cram a whole week of living into every weekend.

41   "Correction — spell it with an *o*!" he grinned wickedly, sobering almost instantly. "Lord, when I think of not having you there to yak with — that's half of loving somebody, the talk and reaching into each other's thoughts."

42   "Half — with an Irishman!" I hooted, and Dave, just as I hoped he would, grabbed for me.

43   We tussled joyously, like a couple of kids, and then as always, our closeness erased everything except the ever-fresh wonder of our love.

44 thru 46: Foreshadowing problem.

44   "Now, there's real communication!" Dave chuckled later, much later, but it wasn't really a wisecrack.

45: Theme.

45   Because underneath all his tomfoolery is a deep-flowing tenderness — that's where our marriage was. If I just hadn't let other things make me lose the sense of its reality!

46   Before then, Dave could've been clear across the country from me, and I wouldn't be lonely. Afterward, to sit in the same

room even wasn't enough to hold back the awful loneliness.

47   Funny, isn't it? So funny it hurts. Terribly!

48   Anyhow, Dave went on to Manning by himself, leaving me with a million instructions — keep the chain on the door, don't go out nights without someone along, phone Tuck if you're in a jam. That sort of thing.

49   "I'm a big girl, remember?" I scoffed at his fussing. "What in the world could happen!"   49: Plant.

50   Actually, I didn't mind his concern. It made me feel safe, and warm, and whole. Beloved. And the way things were working out in his job, it was plain I'd been overly cautious about waiting to move.   50 and 51: Transition — time bridge.

51   In fact, as Dave said when he came in from Manning around midnight Friday, we were as sure now as we'd ever be!

52   "And we certainly ought to be able to afford a baby on my salary too," he'd started almost before he was inside the door. "Give the hospital notice Monday morning, then next Saturday grab the first bus to Manning, and I'll meet you there — we can figure the rest out afterward."

53   Now, everything was changed again, and I'd have to wait to give that notice — actually, I'd only had to take a week off, because Dave snapped out of it so fast. The whiplash injury was a false alarm, according to the doctor in Altamont, and the head contusion was already healed. Even so, he insisted that Dave wear a neck brace on the   53. Coming out of flashback to present.

53 and 54: Research material on medical problem. Plant for

trip home, and for at least ten days afterward.

<small>stroke which creates story problem.</small>

54 "Better be safe than sorry," he advised. "The nerves and tissues in that area have had quite a shock, and a further jolt could cause some temporary impairment — just take it easy, and you should be back at work in another week."

55 "Might as well harness me up and call me Ol' Dobbin!" Dave cracked, rebellious of the thick leather collar that held his chin high, preventing any sidewise movement. "Look, Doc — I've got a radio station to operate, I can't sit around and baby myself!"

56 Bless Tuck though. He'd come up to drive us home, and laid the law down about Dave taking chances with his health.

<small>57: Plant.</small>

57 "You can't be lucky all the time, boy," he reasoned. "Think of Peggy — hasn't she had enough worry already?"

58 But Dave wasn't exactly a model convalescent. Like most men, he fumed and fretted about nothing. Usually ending up with my being gone part of the day.

<small>59 thru 67: Narrator's character flaw and its effect so far brought out through action and conflict of quarrel scene.</small>

59 "That darn job of yours, Peg!" he lashed out one evening while I was in the middle of showing him the stew that was all fixed and ready to be heated for his lunch the next day. "Did you ever count up how much that piddling paycheck has cost us?"

60 "Dave —"

61 "Hospital bills, the doctor, our car smashed — Peg, all you had to do was quit when I asked you, and I wouldn't have been dead for sleep and having to hit the road anyhow!"

62   Without giving me a chance to remind him that we'd discussed the whole thing back at the beginning, Dave stalked out of the kitchen, slamming the door so hard the windows rattled. Hurt, and mad clear through too, I crept into bed to lie wide-eyed, smarting at the unfairness of Dave's attack.

63   And on top of everything else, he'd turned the television on full blast — just being ornery, that's what it was!

Still, I must've dozed off finally, because the next thing I knew Dave was there beside me.

64   "Sorry, baby —" he whispered contritely. "Don't know what got into me — cabin fever maybe."

65   "Sure, darling —" with a contented sigh, and cautious of the brace he still wore, I curled happily against his warm bulk.

66   "As soon as I get out of this harness —" he promised drowsily. "Gosh, I bet you'll look cute in a maternity dress!"

67   It was pitch dark, and deathly quiet, when something jerked me bolt upright, heart plunging wildly. A prowler? Then I saw that Dave's pillow was empty, and relaxed.

68   "Just Dave going to the bathroom," I thought.

69   But no light showed beneath its door, and the stillness was somehow ominous — fear suddenly balled icily in the pit of my stomach.

70   "Dave — darling, are you all right?"

71   Rushing headlong across the room, I pounded on the bathroom door, and when he

67 thru 77: Scene to dramatize Dave's stroke, because this is the medical problem that motivates story problem.

didn't answer, fumbled with trembling fingers for the knob.

72   "Darling — oh Dave, what is it?"

73   Face contorted in the faint light from the hall, he was propped against the washbowl, rigid and unmoving. Only his eyes seemed alive, and as long as I live, I'll see the desperate pleading in that fixed stare!

74   Panicked, I whirled to the phone, and managed to dial St. Joseph's. Somebody there, I guess Admitting, said they'd send an ambulance right away. Staggering back to Dave, I clung to the door jamb, completely exhausted.

75   He hadn't moved so much as a muscle. Pajamas gaping open, and body angled backward, his head reared grotesquely erect above the leather collar. Like — crazily, laughter bubbled in my throat.

76.   "Ol' Dobbin!" I gasped, the hysteria rising. "Harness you up, and — oh Dave!"

77.   Flinging myself against him, I tried to lift his inert-hanging arms around me. And horrified by their dead weight, I began to scream. Jagged, tearing screams that ripped the dread silence to shreds.

78: Transition — time bridge.

78   There's no point in reliving that agonizing wait for the ambulance, nor the hours of crouching in the Nurses Lounge while tests were made, and doctors consulted — it's only a blur anyhow.

79   And so far as their diagnosis goes, I'm still confused by the medical terms tossed at me. All I could catch was that Dave had had a stroke!

80   A stroke — at his age, not even thirty yet!

81   Shocked, not really comprehending, I caught hold of the grave-faced physician's arm. "Doctor, will he —" I faltered, the question clogging in my throat. "Is Dave going to die?"

82   "No, and with therapy, we should be able to establish new brain patterns — in time your husband may recover completely."

83   "Thank God!" I gasped, then another fear struck me. "Brain patterns, you mean his brain is paralyzed — but that's the same as insane, isn't it?"

84   Dr. Benedict sighed. "Mrs. Eagan, I'm going to give you a sedative and send you home," he said. "Perhaps there's someone I can phone for you?"

85   I must've given him Tuck's name, or maybe just the station's call letters. I'm not even sure which, but Tuck got the message. By the time he came though, the sedative was taking hold, and I didn't care whether it was Les Tucker, or the cop on the corner who kept telling me not to worry.

86   "I'll take care of everything —"

87   But how could he? Because *everything* was Dave — and Dave was paralyzed! His whole right side, and when he tried to speak, there was only this awful wordless sound. For days he was like that, and I wasn't even sure he knew it was me.

88   Or knew anything at all!

89   A month flat on his back, and every day physio-therapists manipulated his legs and

80 thru 94: Medical research on stroke causes and therapy techniques for rehabilitation. Shown in scenes and illustrative action.

84 thru 87: Points up closeness of Tuck's relationship with Dave and Peggy.

87 thru 89: Transition — time bridge.

arms. *Passive exercising,* they called it. And always the checking for reactions, and more neurological tests to determine the extent of brain damage.

90 "What made it happen to Dave — why did he have a stroke?" I had to have a definite reason. Something I could put my finger on, and say *this is it, nothing else, only this is to blame.*

91 Oh, I'd read about cholesterol, and the danger of fatty deposits accumulating in your arteries. High blood pressure, too. But Dave didn't have any of those things, he was almost perfect physically — so, why?

92 Dr. Benedict wasn't sure either. He said a tiny clot might have broken loose when Dave hit his head in the wreck, and gradually worked its way up into a small blood vessel somewhere in the brain. It was just speculation though, because if there'd been such a clot, it was dissolved by the time tests were run. The thing is, the night Dave had his stroke, a clot could've momentarily cut the circulation there.

93 "We call that a cardio-vascular accident," the doctor explained. "Any stoppage of blood to the brain also interrupts its supply of oxygen, and if it continues even for a few seconds, certain tissues are damaged — perhaps those that control body movements, or ones in the speech and memory centers."

94 At least, Dave was young, so most of the affected tissues were supple and probably would repair themselves. If it turned out they'd been destroyed — well, therapy might

help him to literally by-pass the dead tissues and build new brain patterns.

95   "Your main concern, however, is the emotional aspects of a stroke," Dr. Benedict warned. "Coping with a CVA victim can disrupt normal family relations, and that's something you must guard against — don't treat your husband as an invalid, and try to be understanding of any personality changes."

96   "I love him, Doctor — Dave can act however he wants, and I won't mind so long as he's getting better!"

97   "Good girl — and don't hesitate to come see me any time," Dr. Benedict suggested, his voice hearty.

98   But as he turned away, there was an expression in his eyes that I didn't wonder about until long afterward. Like he was sorry for me. Like — well, like the way you are if somebody dies!

99   Right then, though, I was just relieved. Because a stroke doesn't have to mean the end of everything, and now that I understood the causes of Dave's paralysis, it didn't seem nearly as hopeless. In fact, there was a lot to be thankful for. We had insurance to cover all this expense of treatment while he was laid up, and even if his sick leave pay wouldn't go on forever, my job here at the hospital would carry us until he got back to work.

100   Another lucky break, the Super assigned me to the floor where Dave was, and let me spend every free minute with him. Besides, she had the therapists teach me the

95: Second half of story "germ" (see Chap. 11, Genesis).

95 thru 98: Foreshadow "muddle."

100 thru 117: Researched medical material on

114   The Confession Writer's Handbook

stroke, and therapy told through action that reader can relate to, or take encouragement. Not necessary to show in fully developed scenes since no pivotal crisis.

101 thru 103: True incident to add reality.

rehabilitation exercises he'd need after he came home.

101   Of course, I did get discouraged sometimes at how slow he was to show the least improvement, but they all kept telling me that it takes time. Then this one day I was sitting beside his bed, and Dave just lay there motionless. A radio was playing in the next room, and I was on the point of going in to turn the volume lower when I could've sworn that I saw the bed covers shift.

102   It was crazy to tiptoe, but for some reason I even held my breath as I edged closer, and lifted the light blanket to peer under it — Dave's right hand was keeping time to the music!

103   I can't possibly describe how beautiful that tap-tap-tap of his fingers was. But if I live to be a hundred, I'll always thrill to the raucous beat of a rock combo!

104   From then on, Dave began to improve fast, and soon he was able to walk down the hall to the bathroom by himself. His right foot dragged pretty badly, of course, and he dropped things put in his hand. But every day showed some improvement!

105   Learning to talk was slower. Over and over, they made him imitate sounds. Not words, only the sound of a letter. The ones like "p" gave him the most trouble, and sometimes he'd get stubborn, just lie there fairly bristling with resentment because he couldn't make his "p's" and "b's" explode properly.

Confession Workshop 115

106   Those speech therapists have the patience of Job though, and gradually he began putting the sounds together. Dave would open his mouth, his throat muscles would work convulsively, and he'd look almost as if he were strangling. It nearly broke my heart to see the struggle he had trying to say the simplest words. The splutters, and how he'd claw the air, as if it was something he could tear loose — and when he finally got them out, the words never had any connection, or meaning!

107   And that really scared me!

108   I guess that's why they say a little knowledge is worse than none. You jump to conclusions, and nine times out of ten come up with the wrong answer. Was Dave's mind gone? There wasn't an hour of the day that I was free of the dread explanation for his labored gibberish.

109   Because the new brain patterns Dr. Benedict talked about were made now — if they weren't, he still wouldn't be able to walk or do almost anything with his body muscles. So, why couldn't you ask him a question, and get an answer that fitted? Maybe the words were too hard to say yet, but he wasn't able to write them either — had the stroke destroyed too much of his brain after all?

110   The thinking part, I mean!

111   When Dr. Benedict came to the Floor on his next rounds, I begged him to tell me the truth, but he seemed to take Dave's condition for granted.

112   "Some form of aphasia is often

106: Plant for cause and effect of problem.

108 thru 111: Foreshadowing fears and frustrations of life with a post-stroke patient.

116 The Confession Writer's Handbook

112 thru 117: Researched medical data on possible aphasia in CVA victim.

present following a CVA," he said matter-of-factly.

113   Then, seeing my bewilderment, he tried to explain *aphasia* by comparing it to something I could follow. According to him, that's the medical term for a gap between the thought and its response. Sometimes the person is able to speak, yet unable to understand what's said. Others can talk and understand but not read, or they read okay, and can't write.

114   With Dave, it was a case of understanding everything that was said, and he could speak and write too — only not the same words his mind communicated to his muscles. Dave's thoughts and his speech centers just wouldn't coordinate yet.

115   "Like tuning in a radio program — the station is broadcasting and your set is in working order, but you must push the right button to get it," Dr. Benedict smiled, and shrugged. "Your husband would say I'm a poor radio man, but that's the general idea — the transmitter and receiver are in good condition, we just haven't provided the proper impulse to open the circuit."

116   "But why can't —"

117   "Because a stroke is similar to any other severe shock, my dear — it takes time to overcome the impact on one's emotions," he reassured. "Even after therapy has succeeded in repairing the actual damage, time is an important factor of recovery."

118   *It takes time* — that was my staff whenever I got discouraged, and I leaned on

Confession Workshop 117

it plenty during the months of nagging frustration after Dave was able to come home from the hospital. Although there was scarcely a sign of paralysis, except in one foot, he still couldn't carry on any kind of conversation. The more he tried, the more it seemed to upset him too, and that's what the doctor said had to be avoided. Emotional disturbances!

119   It's funny how confident I'd been that loving Dave so much was all I needed to cope with things. I know now that love isn't enough, and the best intentions in the world can turn into a nightmare. You think you can understand. You think you can accept. You make plans, and you try to keep calm no matter what happens — but nobody knows ahead of time how they'll react!

120   You have to live with a stroke victim day after day to find that out!

121   In the first place, I'd taken a transfer to third shift, eleven at night until seven in the morning, so I could be home daytimes. But Dave didn't know I was putting in those eight full hours at the hospital every night. I did a lot of thinking about whether or not to tell him, and decided against it. After all, if he couldn't even place a simple question together, how could I expect to discuss the necessity for my working still?

122   I don't believe in a woman sneaking behind her husband's back, but Dave wasn't supposed to get upset, and my job was already a touchy subject. So, no matter how

118: Transition — time and place.

118 thru 126: Stage Three — attempt to cope with situation. Foreshadows later crisis. Narrated — day to day routine important, but no crisis to be highlighted in a scene.

120: Problem stated.

much it went against my grain, I didn't have much choice right now.

123   Even so, if Dave wasn't supposed to have the bed to himself for awhile, I might not have gotten away with the subterfuge. This way though, I had him settled for the night by nine-thirty at the latest, and with the mild sedative Dr. Benedict prescribed, he didn't know whether I was in Timbuktu, or asleep on the davenport!

124   Usually, I closed the bedroom door, and turned the radio low until it was time to dash for the bus. Or sometimes, if Tuck had come by earlier to visit with Dave, he'd stay on, and drive me to work. Either way, I was back home before Dave woke up, and then I'd try to catnap whenever I could during the day.

125   Tired? I was plain exhausted all the time, and the change in Dave's disposition didn't help the situation any. When he first began to get so irritable, I shrugged it off — aren't most men cranky if they even have the sniffles? And Dave was recovering from a serious illness. *It just takes time,* a dozen times a day I'd remind myself that his moods were only temporary, the normal after-effect of a stroke.

126 and 127: Theme — fragmentary flashback.

126   I didn't blame him for getting depressed either. Poor guy, anybody as active and charged with the sheer joy of just being alive was bound to suffer plenty if he couldn't express himself. Because when you can't even ask for a drink of water or comment on what's in the newspaper — well, Dave always

claimed that communication is more important than anything else.

127 "Take us though —" he used to brag, "we talk together with all our senses — that's what counts, instead of just yakking!"

128 But Dave was wrong about one thing — you need to talk with words too! If you can't, there's a silence that drags you down, and no amount of talking with other people helps.

129 Sure, it's easy to hand out advice about not letting yourself get into the dumps, and how there's an emotional effect on the stroke victim's family that has to be watched. Only when you're right in the middle of it, you don't think, or analyze. You just feel.

130 And if I'd had the sense God gives little green apples, I would have gone to Dr. Benedict back at the very beginning, during those first weeks that Dave was at home!

131 But what could I tell him — that every word Dave said was a physical ordeal, and when he finally got it out, utterly meaningless? That sometimes he was fussier than a dozen spoiled kids? That I was tired all the time, and deserved a medal for doing what any wife should if her husband is sick?

132 A busy neurologist like Dr. Benedict — take up his valuable time with things he'd warned me to expect?

133 Only there was one thing we hadn't discussed, and that's the real reason I shouldn't have put off going to him!

134 I was embarrassed to come right out and say Dave hadn't even touched me once

128 and 129: Problem — emotional trauma. Effect on stroke patient's family. Reader identification through identifiable or understandable reactions.

130 thru 132: Character flaw that causes Peggy to reason instead of act.

133 thru 135: Motivation for her not taking decisive

action in time.	in these weeks — or that I could bear the rest, if he'd just make love to me. It was too intimate, too private.
	135 So, I didn't go to the doctor while there was still time to gain the full understanding I'd need desperately. Now, there'll always be that torturing speculation, another *if*.
136 thru 151: Problem becomes crucial — scene dramatizing researched medical aspect of CVA.	136 You see, Tuck called this one evening, and I had barely said "hello" when the receiver was yanked out of my hand. 137 "Dave, for heaven's sake — I've just started to talk!" I snapped, trying to grab it back. 138 But he slammed the phone up anyhow, and stood there, throat muscles working convulsively. Well, I had to hang on tight to keep from exploding. And all the while, Dave was shaking his head at the phone, then he'd point to himself and nod. 139 Talk to him instead, was that what he meant? Talk to him — suddenly I lost control. 140 "It's hard enough this way —" I stormed. "Please, Dave — don't make it a duty too!" 141 Sobbing, I pushed past him to the sofa, but inside I was already contrite for that outburst. I guess Dave was surprised out of his own tantrum too. Slowly, dragging his bad foot, he followed me across the room. And his eyes that used to blaze with those blue flames of excitement were filled with the pain of his isolation.

142 "I didn't mean it, darling — honest, I'm sorry!"
143 Reaching up, I pulled him closer, and his hand brushed my breast as he stooped forward. Instantly the familiar urgency surged through me, and I could feel the pound of Dave's heart, the quick tremor of the sharp-drawn breath that caught in his chest.
144 "Dave —" I gasped, pressing tighter to him. "oh, darling — please!"
145 Then — but I'll never be sure which was first, the shocking flood of obscenities, or the knowing that Dave wasn't really going to make love to me.
146 Couldn't!
147 Yet, his hands still possessed me. Seeking and feverish. And all the while, his voice — Dave, who hardly ever swore even, was mouthing words straight out of the dirtiest gutter anywhere!
148 Twisting loose, I huddled away from him. *Personality changes* — oh God, how can a man change so much!
149 At least, it was the weekend, and I didn't have to go to work in this state. I heard our neighbor's cuckoo clock chime eleven, and twelve, then one o'clock, but I continued to toss, wide awake. Trying to remember other things Dr. Benedict had explained, and that I'd probably only half listened to. And certainly hadn't comprehended.
150 Maybe it was all part of the aphasia — I'd see Dr. Benedict tomorrow, and maybe he would tell me it was just this first time after Dave's having been so sick.

151: Transi-
tion — time
bridge.

152: Transi-
tion —
place bridge.

156: Plant
— incident

151   Tomorrow. Why do we always look to it for comfort? I brought Dave's breakfast to him, and eyes mirroring the shame that weighted my heart too, he drew me down beside him on the bed — it was a repetition of last night, except for the awful language he'd used before. This time he kept his mouth clamped shut, but everything else was the same!

152   "Can he ever — will we be able to —" cheeks flaming, I somehow managed to describe those two futile attempts to Dr. Benedict when I went to his office that morning.

153   He took off his glasses then, and sat tapping them against his palm. The cursing wasn't unusual in CVA cases, he said. Even ministers and gentle old ladies will often start using four letter words every other breath — hating the sound, and unable to stop the flow of profanity.

154   With Dave, it may have even caused the impotency!

"Emotional trauma is unpredictable, but it's usually the cause of any loss of sexual power," the doctor continued. "The stroke itself, the aphasiac condition, and now the cursing last night —"

155   Each was a severe shock to the emotions, and no two people react the same, he said, adding that there's no way to know for sure which had caused this latest complication. Or how long it would last. Psychiatric treatment might even be necessary eventually.

156   "Right now, I'd predict it'll clear when the aphasia does, and that may take

time," Dr. Benedict smiled reassuringly as he got to his feet. "But full recovery can also be dramatically sudden in aphasia cases — sometimes just the right counter-shock will cause a break-through."

that leads to resolution.

157   It was like walking in a fog to come out to the street that was jammed with Saturday shoppers, and carefree couples wandering along in a holiday mood. Their very normalness made what I faced more bleak. Up to now, I'd held my love between, refusing to examine the words that rushed into my consciousness as I plodded toward the bus stop.

157 thru 161: Contrast to point up narrator's despair, and fears for the future of her marriage.

158   What have I got, I thought. A home, a husband?

159   Take how Tuck, and everybody else at the station, was so darned sorry for Dave. Well, they might try being a little sorry for me too!

160   I'd known I must never think about those words, but now my defenses against them had crumbled — because if Dave stayed impotent, our only chance at any sort of closeness was gone.

161   What would be left then, except the empty shell of a marriage — and duty!

162   "Lift, lady?" a gay voice hailed, and I was so sunk, it took a minute to recognize that it was Tuck pulling alongside me.

162 thru 179: Scene dramatizes seeming hopelessness of situation, and motivates narrator's reaction to being left alone,

163   "You're busy, Tuck — I can catch the bus," I finally shook my head.

164   He stared at me thoughtfully, eyes questioning the misery in mine. "More trouble, hmm — how about a good solid listening post?"

165   It was easier to climb in beside him than argue, and sensitive to my mood, he drove silently until we came to a sheltered cove by the river. Settling down on the bank there, Tuck lighted a cigarette.

166   "Okay, Peggy — want to tell me?"

167   But there are certain things you don't discuss with other people, even as close a friend as Tuck was to both Dave and me, *without even Tuck's friendly comfort to lean upon.* Catching on, Tuck switched to something else.

168   "Lucky break, running into you —" he said. "I'm so crowded for time, and I sure would hate to miss saying good-by to you two."

169   "Good-by —?"

170   "For awhile, at any rate — that's what I wanted to tell you when we got disconnected last night, and things piled up so I couldn't call back again."

171   It seems Eagle Broadcasting was considering a hook-up that would add several more stations to the present chain. Tuck was to spend time at each and report how he thought they rated as future Eagle outlets.

172   "You remember Mike Solka, he was at your party — well, he's taking over at KMPC while I'm on the road the next two or three months, might even be longer."

173   "When —"

174   "That's just it, Peggy — I'm ticketed out of here on the 11:05 flight tonight, and maybe you'll have to pass the word on to Dave."

175   "We'll miss you —" I started to say,

like you do if any friend is leaving, and went all to pieces instead.

176   We had so little company nowadays, once the first rush of concern about Dave's stroke wore off, and to have Tuck still drop by meant a lot. But he was going away, and I was tired, and heart-sore, and — anyhow, the tears spilled over, and I couldn't stop crying. Hunched over, I sobbed until there wasn't a tear left in me — only the loneliness that was my life now.

177   Still not prying, Tuck merely handed me his hankie, and reached around to pick up my jacket that had slipped to the ground behind. I don't know exactly how it happened, but I must've turned at the same instant, because my cheek touched his. Then, before either of us could straighten, our lips brushed too.

177. Device that makes the suddenness of adultery logical

178   It wasn't a kiss, just one of those coincidences that you can't help. And I'm no sexpot, no matter how it sounds. But the weeks of longing for my husband's love, and the frustration of its denial twice in succession, somehow balled into a tragic parody of the *aphasia* that had changed Dave too — my body responded to that accidental contact, disregarding the frantic signals of every decent instinct in me!

178: Fragmentary flashback reviewing motivation for infidelity. Note that sex act itself is not graphic, only implied.

179   When Tuck and I drew apart at last, it was forever too late!

180   "Peggy — oh God, Peggy!" he groaned.

181   Spent and shaken, we stared at each other, aghast at what we'd done.

182 thru 184:
Peggy's concern for Tuck is to stir a like compassion in reader for her.

182   "Don't, Tuck —" I said dully. "It wasn't your fault!"

183   Back at the apartment, Tuck scarcely slowed enough to let me out of the car. "Tell Dave I can't —" he broke off, and I glimpsed the shine of tears in his eyes as he shot away from the curb.

184   But I knew what he'd left unsaid. Not that he didn't have time for good-bys, but that his friendship with Dave was over — once you betray a friend, you can't be his friend ever again. That's what he hadn't said!

185   Oh, Tuck sent an occasional postcard, and I hadn't been exactly a ray of sunshine lately anyhow, so between those two things it was fairly simple to keep Dave satisfied. For the time being, that is.

186   Meanwhile, Dave's leg was responding to the daily massage I gave him, and we worked every spare minute on his speech, although sometimes I wondered if he'd ever be able to express himself intelligibly. The words, written or spoken, simply wouldn't connect with what he wanted to say.

187 thru 191:
Narrator attempts to carry on — seeks a way to save her marriage.

187   As for anything more intimate, I tried to reassure him of my love, and at the same time, avoid anything that might rouse passion in either of us.

188   "Let's wait, darling — why take the chance of a set-back when you're almost well!"

189   And I'd paste a bright, sparkly smile on my mouth, with the truth a churning sickness inside me. Sure, when he got well!

Confession Workshop 127

190   Nights, at work, I thought about that time constantly, and the decision I'd have to make then. Hurrying to answer the blinking call lights, rocking a feverish child to sleep, lingering an extra moment with another of the lonely charity patients — it tormented me every waking hour.

191   Because, if you love somebody, there shouldn't be any secrets. Yet, if a man's faith is destroyed, his whole outlook on life is damaged. The more I thought about whether to tell Dave or not, the harder it was to think straight.

192   But, like the old saying goes, *Man proposes, and God disposes!*

193   This one morning I'd just given Dave a postcard Tuck had mailed from Detroit, when all of a sudden I was deathly sick, and almost didn't make it to the bathroom. Probably that tuna sandwich yesterday, I told myself. Or maybe the shortribs at dinner were too greasy.

194   Could be, only I was sick the next morning. I was sick every morning — indigestion seven days a week? Besides, I was way over-due, and up to then had laid it to a cold, or being so upset!

195   Mostly, though, the nausea seemed to hit while I was still at the hospital mornings. But that was okay, since Dr. Benedict was the only outsider who knew Dave and I hadn't been together like that for nearly six months. Not even Tuck would be able to count on his fingers, although he wasn't that kind of person anyhow.

190 and 191: Reader identification strengthened with narrator's inner conflict.

193 thru 200: Further and climactic complication of her pregnancy.

196   But pregnancy doesn't stay a secret long, and it was Dave's reaction that had me half crazy with worry. Because I just couldn't imagine a life without him, and unless I thought of something awfully quick, I'd have to!

197   Sometimes, crossing the street, I almost wished a truck would run me down. But that's as close as I came to thinking of suicide. I loved Dave too much to put him through that kind of hell!

198   It was the same with abortion. You think one of those operations can undo the trouble you're in, but I've seen some of the botched cases brought into Emergency. And even the legalized ones aren't as simple as they sound.

199   The dangers weren't all of it either. In spite of everything, I wanted to keep my baby. Somehow, with that tiny body nestled inside me, and knowing it was there growing to a little boy, or a little girl, I wasn't quite so lonely.

200   Which brought me right back to Dave again — it was such a hopeless situation, and the longer I waited to do something, the worse it got. Every day my breasts were swelling more against a bra that was already too tight, and in the shower, I couldn't help noticing the slight rounding of my stomach — how long before Dave would see those tell-tale changes too?

201   So, it seemed almost the answer to a prayer when I started to rummage for an article I'd cut out about speech blocks, and

ran across an old snapshot of Tuck. Staring at his rumpled dark hair, and the wide-set eyes that were the same steady blue as Dave's, I wondered if the baby would have a dimple in its chin. Both Tuck and Dave did, a real deep one.

202   Funny, how much they looked alike — and suddenly my breath caught. Because it wouldn't really matter if the baby took after Tuck!

203   Delayed pregnancy — why hadn't I thought of it until now?

204   Maybe it sounds wild, but delayed pregnancies are medically possible, and not as rare as you'd think. It happened before I was working there, but they'd even had one case at St. Joseph's. This woman's husband had been killed nearly a year back, yet the doctors all agreed that the baby she had was his. I'm just a practical nurse, and most medical terms are over my head, so I can't explain the why's and wherefore's. The hospital records though, and the regular duty nurses say it's been proved that conception was three months after the couple last had relations.

205   How long a delay is possible? I still don't know, and only cared then that it was a slim hope to preserve Dave's faith, and give my baby a clean start in life!

206   I was smiling for the first time in weeks as I went to tell Dave supper was about ready, and going by, snapped on the radio.

207   "There were no survivors in today's tragic plane crash —" it was right in the mid-

201 thru 205: Possible way to keep both her baby and secret — little known, documented medical fact. Narrator feels that now there's hope of getting out of "muddle."

206 thru 214: Stage Four. Climax—dark moment when

everything falls apart. Shock of Tuck's death, and disclosure of her infidelity to Dave. Narrator's remorse, and attempt to right wrong she's done.	dle of a newscast, and I paused a moment to listen. "Listed aboard were three Pacific Northwest residents — Lester Tucker, Gresham, Oregon, manager of station KMPC —" 208 "The baby —" I didn't know I'd screamed, or that my hand instinctively reached to shelter it. 209 I didn't even feel Dave's fingers bite into my shoulder, or the jolting crack of his palm against my cheek. But I'll never forget the bleak pin-pointing of his eyes, and the utter desolation of hearing the drag of his lamed foot across the floor. Away from me! 210 Dave knew — the time for subterfuge was forever past! 211 For days afterward, he just sat silent, not exercising or anything. Staring into space. Eating the food I set in front of him. Going to bed, and getting up. And the silence was an iron weight in my heart. 212 "I'm sorry, Dave — so terribly sorry," finally I knelt beside him, eyes lowered from the hate and disgust that must be mirrored in his. "When — just as soon as you don't need me here, I'll leave!"
213 thru 219: Countershock which was planted for in Par. 156. Scene dramatizes Dave's break through the aphasia.	213 Now the silence had settled into the air itself, thickening it so I could hardly breathe. But Dave's throat worked convulsively, his face contorted with that labored effort, and the words he couldn't transmit were louder than any spoken ones. 214 Thank god — he can't say them, I thought. At least, I wouldn't have to carry their bitter lash away with me! 215 And in the same instant, Dave's

voice smashed through, a torrent of rushing sound exploding into words.

216 "Need you — always!"

217 "It'll take time, Dave —" I faltered, too sunk in misery to comprehend that his *aphasia* was finally overcome. Suddenly and dramatically, just as Dr. Benedict had said it might happen. "Don't you see, I've got to stay until — I won't bother you any more, but you need me around to help awhile yet."

218 "I do need you, darling — I never really stopped!"

219 I still didn't believe I'd heard right, not until long after Dave had pulled me hungrily close, his lips against my tear-clogged throat.

220 "When I heard what my own voice was saying — the rotten filth coming out of my mouth, instead of how much I love you —" he went back again and again to that shocking night. "Peggy, it was like ramming my head into a stone wall — and you think I don't understand?"

221 "But there's my baby —"

222 "Our baby!" he corrected tenderly. "However he was conceived, he'll be born of our love — don't ever forget that, darling!"

223 Every day since, Dave has proved he wasn't just making talk. I remember his hand holding mine in the labor room the night our little boy came, and his look of awe afterward.

224 "He's got fingernails even!" Dave

215 thru 225: Exemplifies theme — love is understanding and sharing.

220 thru 229: Stage Five. Conclusion. Narrator's understanding of her character flaw, and the emotional trauma of a stroke's effect on the family of the victim — lesson to be learned by reader is anti-climactic, so is kept as brief as possible. Up-beat ending.

marvelled. "Black hair too — y'know, I bet he's going to take after his old man!"

225   And I remember other things. Like the pitcher's mitt for a two-year-old bundle of mischief. Like the snapshots that bulge his wallet, and how David, Jr. already walks with Dave's eager swing.

226   Because good fathers are made by living, not just a moment's passion — and Dave is a good father. The best!

227   The trouble is, I'll always wonder whether I actually brought all that other mess on us myself. It started with Dave's wreck, and I know that wouldn't have happened if I'd been willing to move up to Manning at the very beginning. Well, I stalled about it, and I stalled about having a frank discussion with Dr. Benedict before my own emotional problem got out of control.

228 thru 230: The "take-away" for readers.

228   Of course, I'm lucky Dave is the kind of man he is, but I still wish I'd taken a better look at my own attitude — and done something about it!

229   That's why I keep thinking of other women who may be shilly-shallying the same right now. It's no time for false modesty either, because the effect of a stroke can do all sorts of harm to the family of a CVA victim, and needs professional help to handle.

230   And with it, there's a lot better chance that the family's tomorrows will all become happy yesterdays!

I decided to use the semi-chronological format, because this confession was written to inform readers about the *personality changes* in a stroke victim that may tear a family apart, or permanently scar its members. The narrator's character flaw, therefore — her tendency to get practical at the wrong times — is only incidental to the story's real purpose, and needn't be probed into. So, the logical place to open was just before Dave's accident, using brief or fragmentary flashbacks to fill in lead-up events.

The trick in doing a documentary is to avoid becoming encyclopedic, and to bring out technical information through action — scenes that show it dramatically in easily identifiable situations. This is why I stressed how Dave and Peg always communicated with all their senses. It gave contrast to the nerve-stretching frustrations of her life once his stroke had made any normal communication impossible. The terrible aloneness then, and Dave's shocking attempts to make love could lead into the adultery episode sympathetically, which was essential.

At this point I might have gone in a number of different directions, and still have arrived at a satisfactory resolution that would exemplify the same theme. But adultery gave me an opportunity to develop both the medical and emotional problems more fully, although it did present a writer's problem too: how to justify infidelity without losing the necessary reader empathy.

Under the circumstances — a sick husband, no matter what his incapacities, ruled out an affair — it had to "just happen." And credibly. I filled my wastebasket before the right incident and device occurred to me!

I felt, too, that Peg should become pregnant as a result of that moment's abandonment. Not with any idea of the old-time *wages of sin,* but to underscore the very real need for an understanding of strokes in general, and to reassure that there is always hope of a full recovery.

Tuck, of course, had to be eliminated. While the manner I chose could've seemed contrived, by establishing beforehand that he'd be flying around the country for the next few months, the fatal plane crash was made to serve a double purpose. It removed Tuck in an acceptable way, as well as providing the second shock Dr. Benedict had said might jolt Dave out of *aphasia,* and in this case, its side-effect of impotency.

Except for these — adultery, Peg's pregnancy and Tuck's death — the other incidents and complications practically created themselves from the stroke situation. I merely used the cause and effect method of plotting discussed earlier, *if* and *what.*

Now, in studying our workshop story, watch how the *Miracle Word* is spelled out through the continuing action and reaction of the characters involved. Can you put your finger on a phrase and say it's the letter "E," or the *reader identification* "I" represents, or the "R" of *reality?* Perhaps, but not often. You see, the confessional elements shouldn't be obvious, and they never stand alone. Each is a part of the whole, and too tightly woven together with the "little things" of daily life to separate one from the other.

Finally, I want you to take particular note of how the necessary medical information actually creates the story line, and causes the dramatic conflict that keeps its forward movement fast-paced.

This last is very important, because all confessions are really only short stories, but dullness is a special hazard in the documentary. And a challenge to you, as the writer!

Chapter Thirteen

Small Packages

Most magazines publish a few very short confessions — ones that can be run on two facing pages with an illustration. These short-shorts are a useful aid in putting an issue together, serving as a kind of "filler" when editorial material and advertising can't be laid out to fit the allocated number of pages without leaving awkward holes. But the late Bruce Elliott, editor of Macfadden-Bartell's *True* Romance Group, saw them as stories in their own right, and began featuring a bonus section of *mini-confessions*.

So, another area is now open to the confession writer, one that's well worth exploring. First, however, let's get this clear — the mini-confession is not an enlarged incident, or a quivering slice of life! It contains all the elements of a full-length confession, but averages only 2,500 words, give or take 500.

Easy — just ten pages to write? Well, it isn't hard — that is, it isn't hard to type ten pages. But to write a good mini-confession is something else again. In the standard lengths, running 4,000 to 7,500 words, you have space to characterize and to motivate, and with a foreshadowing of complications to come, can lure the reader deeper into your narrator's problem. Yet in the tight fit of a 2,500-worder, you still must establish *character, problem, motivation* and *reader identification* — everything necessary to untangle the knots a confused narrator may have tied in her life or attitudes. You must get in the mini-confession frame of mind before so much as a word is written.

While the same idea might be developed in a full-length story, the mini writer will probe into it from a different angle — often philosophical — with emphasis on the *art of living*. Because that's what confessional short-shorts really are, fictional counterparts of those self-help articles.

Remember, however, mini-confessions are not mere condensations. They have all the essential qualities of regular confessions, but right from the start are written to the shorter length, every sentence, phrase or word doing triple duty — each chosen to characterize, further the action and develop theme. So, it is necessary to always search for the picture-making word, the noun that releases associations in a reader's mind, the verb which doubles as an adjective. As an example, suppose we have a man sitting on a park bench . . .

If he *springs* to his feet, the reader sees that he's young and vigorous; if he *eases* to his feet, we have the picture of an old, or perhaps ill man. And when the narrator watches a woman *plod* toward her, she's probably fat, tired — and determined. Just one very small, but powerful verb, denotes a lot of information.

On the other hand, when a 6,500-word confession is stripped to its bones and re-told in a couple of thousand words, you have a *synopsis* — or an outline, or sketch, or episode — certainly not a mini-confession. You see, ideas for these must be distilled and double-distilled. Each time you throw away excess wordage, the concentrate becomes stronger. This is the distinctive thing about mini-confessions — they're *story concentrates*.

Now, let's take an idea that nagged at me for quite a long while, and I'll show you how I finally worked it into the mini-confession we're going to use for our second Workshop story. . . .

At 87, my grand-aunt had outlived almost everybody who'd been close, with a nephew and me the only family she left. Her pitifully short funeral procession had stopped for a traffic signal, and just as it changed to orange, a woman darted out from the curb, cutting in between our car and the hearse to beat the light.

Doesn't anybody care, I thought bitterly. It was then that I saw an elderly black man, grizzled head bared to the pelting rain, and sodden hat held to his heart. As we rolled past, his eyes met mine, and — well, I couldn't afterward forget the compassion in them. I kept seeing that picture, but it wasn't until much later my own bleak questioning began to seem a story possibility. *Doesn't anybody care?* Yes, but not enough — and from some pigeonhole of my mind came those moving lines of James Russell Lowell's in *The Vision of Sir Launfal*:

> The Holy Supper is kept, indeed,
> In whatsoever we share with another's need,
> Not what we give, but what we share, —
> For the gift without the giver is bare,
> Who gives of himself with his alms feeds three —
> Himself, his hungering neighbor, and me.

There it was, my theme, *not what we give, but what we share, for the gift without the giver is bare.* The shabby old man who had cared enough to share the grief of a stranger was, of course, its embodiment. He'd given the extra that makes a full measure, and as far back as I could remember, so had my grand-aunt.

But weren't they exceptions — little things, maybe only a minute's time, yet pressured by the hurry-flurry of daily life, don't most of us short those we care for?

That's why I can't ever forget Aunt Tottie, now I was

mulling it over to myself on the typewriter, *or the stranger who took the time to care enough that day of her funeral. Somehow, I think God was there too!*

I knew that I had my story's wrap-up, and with it on paper, I was ready at last to write the rest. You see, while the *opening* always stems from the *end,* this familiar rule refers to a problem's resolution, and in mini-confessions that means the actual closing incident.

Why the difference? Well, their very length makes it possible to blunt the point of a longer confession, but without that extra space to move around in, the mini's point must be particularly sharp and penetrating. And by writing the *ending* first, this stronger focus is achieved.

Obviously, I couldn't just write about my regrets after it was too late, or I would've wound up with a maudlin detailing of the blame I'd heaped on myself. Also, although I was creating a fictional *Aunt Tottie* in my own grand-aunt's image, what I wanted to say would have greater impact if I stayed out of the telling. Or rather, if I climbed inside someone who wasn't bound to her by ties of kinship. Perhaps a neighborhood youngster who takes her for granted, too busy with growing up to be aware of a kindly old woman's loneliness.

I dug deeper into my childhood then, recalling nostalgically the small variety store where we used to make as much over a nickel's worth of candy as I do choosing a new dress today. The striped dog-eared sacks of peanuts that were a Sunday treat after church let out. The scent of honeysuckle, and the comfortable creak of Mrs. Hanrahan's old-fashioned rocker on warm summer evenings. And always I came back to that man who had *cared enough.*

The workshop story that follows will show you how a clutter of unrelated memories can be woven into a 2,000 word confession with significance and strong reader identification.

Chapter Fourteen

Mini-confession Workshop

"The Full Measure"

Reprinted by permission of Macfadden-Bartell, Inc. from *True Experience*

1   Aunt Tottie. She wasn't really anybody's aunt, only the name seemed to fit, and it's what two generations of us had always called her. Besides, without the heart of an aunt she wouldn't have tolerated the big deal neighborhood youngsters made of spending their pennies on cheap candies. No matter how long it took to decide between the relative lasting quality of a licorice whip compared to jawbreakers, Aunt Tottie didn't lose patience.

2   "Two of those, and some of these, and —" we used to range back and forth in front of her candy case, calculating greedily. "Golly, Aunt Tottie — don't you have any chews left?"

3   She'd smile that twinkly smile of hers, just as if this sale was more important than any other. "And one to come back on —" she always popped another goodie into the sack before giving it a twirl to make fat ears at the top.

4   That's how she treated grown-up customers too, and whether it was cutting an

1 thru 4: Stage One. Characterization.

4: Theme.

extra half yard of muslin for good measure, or weighing heavy on a pound of tenpenny nails, Aunt Tottie usually gave more than she got.

5 thru 15: Stage Two.

5   Of course, ours is a tight, almost small-townish community, the kind where folks raise their families in the same houses they were born in themselves. Most of our dads worked in downtown Seattle, or the other side of town at Boeing Aircraft, but except for that, you'd hardly know the Wallingford district was part of a big city. Maybe that explains Aunt Tottie, and how close we all were to each other.

6   At any rate, when she finally had to close her small variety store, everybody worried right along with her, the same as if a member of the family was having trouble. I was only eight then, and too young to understand much of it, but there was talk that the wholesalers might even take her house for the accounts she owed. Maybe the law wouldn't have let it come to that, but before any legal action could be started, a lot of the men got together, and worked out a settlement with Aunt Tottie's creditors.

7: Foreshadowing.

7   Dad was one of those who dug down in his pocket, and Mom didn't say a single word about his needing the money for a new overcoat, or that groceries were higher than a cat's back these days. What I mean, nobody had to be shoved into giving a hand when there was an emergency. They all wanted to, and were willing to make personal sacrifices if it'd help the old shopkeeper get straightened out.

Mini-Confession Workshop 141

8   "Not a hundred dollars of stock left on the shelves, and bill collectors ready to grab anything that wasn't nailed down," I remember Dad fuming, and then his eyes softened, "She's going to be lonesome as heck without customers to pass the time of day with — why don't you stop by and say hello when you get time, hon?"

9   "Of course, I will — the poor dear living there all alone," Mom nodded, looking like she was on the edge of crying.

10   Aunt Tottie was a mighty independent woman, however, and disliked being a burden to others. But the store fixtures, and some other odds and ends, brought a better price than was expected, so she didn't have to *feel beholden* after all, as she put it.

10: Characterization.

11   With that off her mind, and a social security check coming in regularly, she seemed to really enjoy taking it easy, and just puttering around the house.

12   As soon as her simple housekeeping chores were done each day, she'd tie on a fresh-starched apron and take a chair out to the front porch where the blue morning glories tangled with wild, sweet honeysuckle. Toward dusk, or if the weather was bad, Aunt Tottie would go indoors to sit by the bay window overlooking the street, rocking comfortably, or leaning forward to wave at passersby.

12: Imagery.

12 thru 13: Action.

13   I've seen her hundreds of times like that, always quick to wave as I raced past on the way to school, and always with the same twinkly smile she'd had when she miscounted the number of chews to a penny, or the thirty-

13: Foreshadowing.

142 The Confession Writer's Handbook

14: Imagery. Transition in time.

15 thru 16: Symbol of theme. Plant.

17: Stage Three. Character flaw.

six inches in a yard of cloth. Then, with a quiet kind of dignity, Aunt Tottie would settle back, hands folded in her lap again as if their usefulness were over now.

14   Gradually, the years crackled the grayish paint of her house, the salt-laden winter winds flaking it off to patches of bare board, and with all the hurry-flurry of growing up, Aunt Tottie became just somebody I waved to whenever I saw her out there on the porch.

15   So, it gave me a sort of funny feeling to have her send me a graduation present. I'd included her on my list for commencement announcements, of course, but I certainly didn't expect Aunt Tottie to even remember my name, let alone give me anything. But a couple of days later the postman brought a lumpy, string-knotted package of penny candies, and those colored balls of gum that she used to carry.

16   "And one to come back on — can't you just hear her saying it?" Mom watched me open the strange little gift that was obviously a somewhat beaten left-over from Aunt Tottie's store. "You mustn't forget to thank her, Barbara."

17   What I really meant to do, was go see her, and make a big fuss about how much I'd enjoyed the goodies, but before I got around to it, this job came up in a downtown insurance firm. So, between the whirl of senior activities, and the excitement of landing a job right out of school, I only had time for a quick note.

Mini-Confession Workshop 143

18   Then, out of a clear sky, the department I was working in was suddenly transferred to the company's regional branch in Portland. Well, you don't go tossing a good job over, even if it does mean a two hundred mile move. That's what I told Mom and Dad when they objeted to my being so far away. They finally agreed it'd be okay, and whenever Dad had a few days of overtime coming to him, they'd drive down to see me. It was on one of those trips that some crazy fool tried to pass a line of cars on the freeway and crashed into them head-on!

18: Transition (time and place).

19   Their funeral and our emptied house afterward, without Mom bustling around the kitchen, or Dad to swing me high in his arms like he'd done since I was knee-high to a cricket — I still can't talk about any of it. I don't even know how I got through the ordeal of sorting and packing their cherished possessions, and I'd probably never have managed if it hadn't been for the neighbors who pitched right in to help.

19: Fragmentary Flashback.

20   Mostly I just worked in a thick, impenetrable fog of grief, and half the time the voices of the others who happened to be there were a blur of sounds to me, not words at all. Like the afternoon Mrs. Donovan and Marge Andrews were in the bedroom below, while I was busy with the accumulation of stuff that had been shoved out of sight in the attic.

21   "Dave says he'd gone a dozen blocks before it hit him that she hadn't waved back when he honked —" Mrs. Donovan was

telling Marge, and although I didn't bother to listen, scraps of their conversation drifted up to me through the floor register.

22   I think it was Marge who said something about its being a nice way to go, just to rock yourself to sleep, but it wasn't until hours later that what they'd been saying finally penetrated. I'd been trying to cram a little more into an already over-full trash can, and this one box toppled out, spilling licorice bits and gumdrops every which way.

23   "Aunt Tottie —" I thought, and in the same instant knew that they'd said she was dead.

24 thru 25: Stage Four. Symbol that foreshadows recognition of character flaw.

24   Staring down at the litter of stale candy, I remembered the day it came, and how Mom had recalled about Aunt Tottie's *one to come back on* — was that what this was? One to come back on?

25   Maybe grief makes a person more sensitive, but thinking of Aunt Tottie now, and the way she always waved to everyone who went by, I began to wonder if she wasn't really keeping an alert watch for possible company besides. Company that never seemed to have a minute to *come back,* no matter how often she might be in a person's thoughts.

26 thru 29: Theme.

26   The trouble is, just being a family fills every chink of time, and nobody ever quite got around to fitting the old shopkeeper into their too-busy days — her health was good, she wasn't in need or anything like that, and later on there'd be more time for a visit!

27   I know Mom used to count the years since Aunt Tottie closed her store, and exclaim at how fast they'd gone.

28   "As soon as I finish my preserves —" Mom would promise herself, or if we took a drive on Sunday, Dad might mention that we ought to ask Aunt Tottie along sometime.

29   I suppose my folks weren't the only ones either, it's just how things go — too much to do, and not enough time for everything!

30   "Don't go tearing yourself apart, lovey," Mrs. Donovan cautioned when I phoned to ask about the funeral. "Just send flowers, and maybe say a little prayer for her."

31   I wanted to take her advice. I was afraid of being forced to re-live the pain of saying good-bye to Mom and Dad, of suffering again the anguish of their tragic deaths. Yet, I couldn't stop thinking of that packet of childish goodies — and wondering!   *31 thru 32: Recognition of character flaw.*

32   The feeling I had was too vague to pin down to any definite reason, more like sensing that even my own folks had failed somehow, that there was something all of us were overlooking — a blindness to some little thing that might make all the difference.

33   At any rate, no matter how much it hurt, I knew I'd have to go to the funeral — perhaps it was only because Mom would've wanted me to.

34   When I got there, the chapel was fragrant with masses of spring flowers, and quite a number of Aunt Tottie's old-time customers had come besides. But as soon as   *34 thru 35: Theme.*

the brief service was concluded, they filed past the casket and hurried off.

35 thru 43: Stage Five. Conclusion.

35   "Want a lift home, Barbara?" Marge Andrews called to me, but I shook my head, determined to go out to the cemetery as well. Maybe it doesn't make sense, yet that seemed awfully important, like doing it for Mom and Dad — the *next time* they'd never quite gotten around to themselves.

36 thru 40: Incident that brings about understanding.

36   Rain was sluicing down by then, and with my own loss heavy within me, the aloneness of death was almost unbearable. Cars kept whizzing by, every driver heedless of the somber hearse, and our pitifully short procession of mourners.

37   "It isn't fair — doesn't anybody care?" I stared resentfully after one woman who had cut directly in front of us, trying to beat the signal light.

38   It was then that I saw him!

39   Just a shabby, stooped old man, he stood there on the street corner, head bared to the storm. But gnarled black fingers held a rain-sogged hat to his breast, and his dark eyes were tender with all the compassion of an entire race.

40   "Thank you —" I whispered as we moved slowly past him.

41: Lesson to be learned.

41   At the moment I was too numbed to see beyond his simple gesture of respect. When my own grief had eased somewhat, however, I thought again of the total stranger who was willing to put himself out for somebody else — to give of himself, you might say.

42   And because he had taken the time

to do it, I began to understand about the extra that makes a full measure — only a few minutes of our time, yet without that extra giving of one's self, aren't we shorting those we care for?

42 thru 43: The Takeaway.

43   That's why I can't ever forget Aunt Tottie, or the stranger who took the time to care enough that day of her funeral — somehow, I think God was there too!

With only 2,000 words to work with, my chief concern was how to bring the theme into sharp focus without seeming to preach. I didn't have room for fully developed scenes, but the idea that our daily lives chip away at good intentions, and most of us *don't take time to care enough* for others had to come through loud and clear. So, I made Aunt Tottie a kindly old storekeeper who always gave more than a full measure, using her characteristic "and one to come back on" to write between the lines. The penny candies seemed a natural to symbolize the giving of herself, and to point up our common human failure to give a similar full measure except in times of emergency.

Ordinarily, too, letting death be the resolving factor is wrong in the confessions. But here I had a true incident — the lone trip out to the cemetery — that illustrated my theme with considerable emotional impact, and readers could identify with that guilty feeling of having waited too long to *care enough.*

In studying the marginal notes in "The Full Measure," you'll see that most of them concentrate on theme, and if you will go back to Chapter Five — *Opening and Ending* — I think it'll be clear why my original philosophical opening was properly blue-penciled out. Those two paragraphs would have weakened the story's message by making it redundant, and destroyed a gentle build-up of suspense that gave impact to the final scene.

The mini-confession is not easy to write, but it's a form that does have broad marketability. I hope you'll try some of these "small packages" yourself.

Chapter Fifteen

Marketing

So, now you're there, ready to type up a final draft and put that confession in the mail. But first, check through once again:

Is the story problem universal, and of enough significance to carry the wordage? How about motivation, narrator's character flaw and theme? Does the opening stem from the ending, and will the reader gain something from this "true" experience? Have you applied the component principles of the *Miracle Word,* and made proper use of those crafting tools?

While the readership of an individual magazine plays a big part in the sales potential of any story, editors all read the yarns that come across their desk with these questions in mind. So, if you'll look at yours objectively, the chance of rejection is lessened. And this is not negative thinking, just good sense!

Next, you'll need a generalized guide to confession marketing — one that will be as useful next year, or the year after, as it is today. For current needs of individual magazines, refer to the specialized listings monthly in *Writer's Digest,* and annually, in *Writer's Yearbook* or *Writer's Market.* These publications all provide a comprehensive coverage of market requirements, and should be considered a necessary reference tools for the serious confession writer.

However, there are areas and factors of marketing that remain fairly constant year after year, yet are too diversified to be taken up in these publications.

For instance, when you sell a confession, endorsement of the check ordinarily releases all rights. But what about the possibility of TV later, reprints in a foreign market, or the novelizing of that story? Does your original release of the material cut off any chance of those residual goodies?

Usually, the rights for such uses will be returned upon request. But where a confession publisher also puts out paperbacks, or perhaps has broadcast interests, then your sale may be final all the way around. Since you can't be expected to know everything about an individual company's policy, a brief letter stating the rights you're requesting is again in order. The worst that can happen is a refusal. And even the magazine that generally holds all rights may be willing to make an exception.

Now, I've mentioned reprints in foreign markets. This is not a fertile field, nor are rates comparable to those of American publications. But if you're interested, there is occasionally an Australian magazine in the market for reprints, and Canada has from time to time had confession magazines that welcome original submissions. As a rule, *when* and *if,* editors from these two countries will list their needs in the "letters" column of *Writer's Digest.* Also, your local library may have a reference copy of *Writers & Artists Year Book* (published by Adam and Charles Black — 4, 5 & 6 Soho Square, London, W.1), which is an excellent source of information on United Kingdom markets in general.

When it comes to the English market specifically, though, confession writers get a break. The London firm of IPC Magazines Ltd. publishes two confession books, *Hers* and *True,* and maintains a New York office (listed in your *Writer's Market*) which screens submissions for forwarding to England. Both are open to the same type of first-person problem stories featured in American magazines, although written with more restraint.

However, you must watch the difference in English idiom. Over there, they turn on the "telly," put luggage in a car's "boot," and park at the "kerb," just as examples. The most frequent reason for rejects at IPC is "use of language only an American audience could understand or respond to," and too American a setting since, "We are English and prefer situations our readers can identify with, e.g. United Kingdom or the Continent." And it may be well to note, too, that reports here take up to six months due to the relaying of scripts overseas. Payment varies, and is determined by the London office, but is usually on acceptance.

Confessions are probably the friendliest of any short fiction market, and editors of individual magazines work with their writers on a more informal basis. But, a precautionary word: don't abuse that closer editor-writer relationship. It does not give you license to trespass on an editor's crowded schedule with your worries about little Suzie's preference in playmates, or where on earth the money is coming from to pay a hefty hospital bill. Tell it in a story, not a letter!

Should you market through an agent? I can't answer that, because it's a matter of personal choice, and whether you have the fortitude to keep scripts in the mail without getting discouraged by repeated rejections. All I can tell you is that every story submitted will be read, regardless of its source, and while an agency folio may get a faster reading, good confessions sell either way.

In fact, going "over the transom" even has advantages — you learn by rejects. Literally! I can't explain why, but I do know that the unhappy sight of a thick manila envelope, and the printed rejection slip tucked inside, gradually builds up awareness in the writer. A sense of what the confession market is, and how to meet its exacting demands. While that sounds odd, and you'll have to take the word of selling pros for it, it is true. Then if you decide later to use an agent, it will be on a sounder basis. Agents want salable yarns, and you'll have learned to pre-judge yours.

Writer's Market lists accredited literary agents, but keep this in mind: the confession market is highly specialized, and not all agents are familiar enough with it to represent you effectively. A few, however, are recognized as specialists in the confession, and I'd recommend making a choice among these in preference to even the most prestigious agency that handles the first-person problem story as an accommodation, or a sideline to other forms of fiction. For their names, your most reliable source is the Market Editor of *Writer's Digest,* or a query to some of the confession editors themselves may give you this information.

One other suggestion, if you decide to continue submitting direct, you might want to check into *The Society of Confession Writers* (P.O. Box 33, Adams, Nebraska 68301), which offers a good many services to the confessioneer for a nominal membership fee.

Now, what about overly delayed reports on submissions? How long should you wait before querying? If you haven't already discovered by experience the time a particular magazine takes, I'd be inclined not to query too soon — you might make up the editor's mind for him! Unfortunately, the lag between submission and reject or sale is lengthening. *Modern Romances* and *Dauntless Books* are presently the only ones that pass on scripts in a fast two weeks from the date of receipt. A few magazines, such as the *KMR Group,* usually report within four weeks; at Macfadden-Bartell it varies with the individual magazine. As an example, *True Romance* averages four weeks, and at the top-pay *True Confessions,* three months is allowed. While these long waits can be hard on fingernails, rather than querying, my advice is to concentrate on turning out new stories and let the mailbox watch itself!

Which brings us to mailing — what class is best? Cheapest is *Special Fourth Class, Manuscript Rate.* However, unless the cost is going to limit your submissions, I'd think twice before trying to save postage at the possible expense of time and handling care. As a clerk at our local post office told me, "It'll get there okay, but how or when is anybody's guess." So, *First Class* both ways is usually preferable, especially now, since First Class really means you'll be getting the old Air Mail service.

For foreign submissions, including Canada, *International Reply Coupons* must be clipped to your self-addressed return envelope. These are available at any post office, which will also verify the appropriate postal rate.

And what kind of stories are you going to submit to this wide-open market? Actually, the confession is the same as it has always been, except as necessitated by changes in today's social system. Legalized abortion, for instance, obviously calls for a different approach to the problem of pregnancy, just as premarital sex is no longer arbitrarily shameful. In fact, it's difficult to define "Sin" nowadays, and confessionally, the *mistake* has been substituted. After all, if these stories are to fulfill their purpose, they must be contemporary, mirroring the current scene honestly.

Although the modern confession reflects present day mores and the ways in which we react to them, most readers are fairly conservative. So, despite the New Morality syndrome, sexual liberation should not be used as the flag on a bandwagon. Interestingly, too, it's beginning to show through that beneath the anti-establishment attitude of young people today there's a strong current of romanticism, and it'll be worth the confession writer's while to watch this trend shape up.

Meanwhile, both types of stories are needed — those

with elements that can be converted into strong cover blurbs, and those that warm the heart. So, take your choice and write either kind. "The challenge is simply this," *Modern Romances'* editor observed in a recent market letter, "a story that can't serve as a cover blurb has to be, quite frankly, a better story than the one that can. Which means it's harder — although probably more interesting to write."

As for subjects, they still run the gamut of human experience, but within the limits of good taste. Medical advances are always good, and so is mental health, or problems related to the "exceptional child" if well researched. There's also an upswing in the supernatural, but stay clear of ghost stories and gothics for the confession market. And, of course, the family story is timeless.

Taboos? If you study several current issues of the magazines you're aiming for — and you always should before submitting to get a clearer idea of what those particular editors might want — you'll find that the only thing taboo is bad taste. Even incest, while I haven't seen it used as a confession problem, might conceivably be handled with sympathy and understanding. Certainly, the prostitute has appeared a number of times, at least once as a minister's wife!

Can sex be delved into clinically? Yes, but not exploited. If a young couple sets up housekeeping without the formality of a marriage license, the problems they face are similar to those of a less free-thinking twosome. Money, unwanted babies, compatability, family interference, sexual hang-ups, religion — anything which may develop from an intimate man-woman relationship.

What's taboo here is the soapbox!

You don't climb onto one, either for or against such "shacking up." It's simply there, and you concentrate on the story problem with the life-style of persons involved incidental, unless that happens to be the problem your narrator is attempting to resolve.

When a couple goes to bed together, you say so. You may play up the girl's emotional response to her lover beforehand, too, although the sex act itself will probably always be blanketed under the mere statement, "We made love."

All in all, it comes down to a remark George Jean Nathan once made, "There are no dirty subjects," he said, "only dirty writers." And if the writer is motivated toward the porno, the confessions are not a showcase for his wares. It's as simple as that.

In general, lengths are becoming shorter, with five to seven thousand words an average. Rates run from 3¢ to 5¢ a word, although some magazines pay a flat price regardless of length, and a few stair-step rates — three to five thousand words brings $175, and then up to seven thousand words — $250. Payment is mostly on acceptance, but the delays in processing may at times seem to contradict this. There's no cause for concern though, as long as you're submitting to established magazines. So-called salvage books can be a different matter, since they come and go, often folding between issues.

Now, what about rejects? The results of an editorial survey show the following as the most frequent reasons for turn-downs:

1. A passive narrator, one who is the victim of circumstances rather than herself, isn't acceptable.
2. Characters are characterless — stock types, so lacking in individuality the reader just doesn't care what happens to them.
3. The story is largely narrated, instead of written in vivid scenes that draw readers into the action.
4. Errors in medical or technical material — sloppy reasearch.
5. Bad writing that takes too much editorial effort to salvage.

6. Hackneyed, predictable plots that lack a fresh approach to spark them.
7. Routine development and contrived climaxes — auto accidents, fire and flood may create drama, but they aren't resolutions to a confession problem.
8. Lack of feeling — the story is emotionally bankrupt.
9. Too explicit sex — the confession never explores sexual activity clinically.
10. Crime glorification — it doesn't pay off.
11. Unsuitable material for the confessions. You must read the confessions to write for them.
12. No theme — the plot is created for itself alone, not to exemplify a lesson to be learned.
13. Not believable — weak motivation and unrealistic.
14. Unsympathetic narrator — spoiled, spiteful, selfish, amoral, deformed physically or mentally — the reader doesn't want to identify with her.
15. Narrator is a bystander, and someone else's problem is really the heart of the matter.

If you recognize a homing story's flaw here, put it back in the typewriter, then "sin" no more! Because it's obvious from this compilation of their comments, confession editors discourage over-sensationalism and the pornographic. They look for strong, believable situations that are handled with freshness and excitement, enabling the reader to become emotionally involved.

"Readers are nice, average women who readily empathize with our stories," editor after editor points out, "and if you can bring a lump to the reader's throat, or get a chuckle out of her, we need you to write for us."

Chapter Sixteen

Confessioneer's Scrapbag

My grandmother's attic was a wondrous place to forage through on rainy afternoons — stacks of old magazines, dome-covered trunks of finery saved from another age for heaven only knows what, button jars, dust-sheeted bureaus and marble tops. And best of all to a sedulous magpie of a child like myself, a muslin flour sack bulged with odd pieces of soft woolens, plushy velvet, and sprigged dimity. I used to dream over that scrapbag by the hour. Handling, matching colors and textures, imagining.

Well, the treasures there have long since been carted off by a junk dealer, and Gram's attic exists only in my heart today. But I have a scrapbag of my own now, and among its tumbled oddments there may be a bit of this or that you'll find useful. Quotes for inspiration, ideas, and just laughs. Answers to some of the puzzling questions a confessioneer runs up against. Tips and techniques. Maybe even a left over dream or two . . .

Confession Writer's Credo

1. I will not bend to the pecking order of status-worshippers who weigh only the by-line.

2. I will not envy, neither my peers in the Confession, nor any writer, no matter how exalted.

3. I will at all times strive to inspire without preaching,

to instruct without boring, and to entertain without pandering.

4. I will not condemn, because I know we don't all march to the same drummer.

5. I will write no word that shames me, but always write proudly.

6. I will not make false promises, nor lead my readers astray.

7. I will give of myself in all that I write, for only then can I help others to help themselves.

8. I will not shut myself away from life, but neither will I go forth to it blindly.

9. I will not use anonymity as an excuse for license, nor put money ahead of integrity.

10. I will not forget that God made us all, nor that we each bear the stamp of all mankind.

How Others Work

Can you earn a living at 3-5¢ a word? I can't answer for you as an individual, but among my confession writing friends is a woman who has raised two children, carried the heavy medical expenses of a permanently disabled husband, and is banking a comfortable cushion for the retirement she'll never take.

She works full-time, nine to five Monday through Friday, with an hour off for lunch and two fifteen-minute coffee breaks. To her, it's a job, and she works at it as one.

I have another friend who goes at it a bit differently. She's on call with Manpower, a business service that supplies part-time and temporary office workers on a commission basis. This way, her hours are more flexible, and whenever confession sales are good, she lays off and concentrates on building up a backlog to circulate during "back to work" interludes. However, she is single and can risk an unsteady income.

Other confessioneers hold down regular jobs, writing nights or weekends. I know a number of housewives, too, who write salable confessions between changing diapers and the family ironing.

Can you earn a living in confessions? Many writers do, and equally as many regard their output as only supplementary to regular sources of income. But whichever group you belong in, confession sales don't drop like manna from above. You have to work for them, even if your writing is merely a hobby!

*

I've found that when I come to an impasse, and everything else has failed, a little *purple writing* will usually bridge the gap. But use this sparingly, and only to complete the illusion when legitimate things are out.

*

Given health, writers never have to retire. 65 is just a number to them, not a cut-off age. I know one confessioneer who, at 78, is still an up-to-the-minute teenager in the stories she sells regularly. Her only concession to age (or perhaps it's for comfort's sake alone) is that all her writing is done in a king-sized bed, with a specially built lap-table that's full width to accommodate typewriter, papers, and an always-filled thermos of coffee.

Just Snips

One of the secrets of successful confession writing is to *see everything as though for the first time*. Only then can it appear to readers in all its newness for the story's narrator.

*

What are we? Walking question marks, that's what, just plain snoops. Like a friend of mine once said, "Gosh, I'd hate to live next door to a confession writer!"

*

All confessions have one thing in common: readers feel that it really happened, and through the intimacy of sharing, that it happened to them.

*

To write confessions you must have the glow of an

enormous love of all people, and a deep faith in the ability of men and women to manage their own lives and happiness.

*

Shopping list picked up in a supermarket and printed by a local newspaper columnist:
>Pot roast
>Scouring powder
>Can hot sauce
>True Confession

*

"It may be corny," a fellow problem-solver explained why she stayed put, "but confessions are a window to life, and I feel blind when I'm away from it."

*

Each confession you write is a new beginning, and all confessions start the same way — with a blank sheet of paper.

Tell Me...

Will Confessions spoil my writing for other fields? Not at all. Confessions make use of every basic fiction principle, emphasizing characterization. If anything, these first-person problem stories will improve your writing technique. In fact, within my own experience, I've known of confessions that wound up bylined in the slicks without any change. And I know one writer who recently sold nine slick-written shorts to top confession magazines — also with no significant changes being made.

*

What can the confession market offer me? Whether fiction will eventually make a come-back in general circulation magazines remains to be seen, but thirty-five confession magazines are currently running an average of seven to eight short stories an issue at rates topped only by the slicks. In addition to this lively sales potential, confessions give a thorough grounding in the psychology of human behavior, a plus in any fiction form. As for competition, *name* means nothing in this unbylined market place. You sell because you've written a good yarn, not because of who you are.

*

Must confessions always be tear-drenched to sell? No, even humor that's written within the confessional framework has a market today.

*

What sort of person is most likely to succeed in confessions? An extrovert, one who genuinely likes people, and is never too busy to exchange confidences, or lend a helping hand when it's needed.

*

If the writer knows somebody with an interesting story in her life, must consent be obtained to use it for a confession? Only if it is to be used "as is," which isn't advisable, since that would involve too many other persons as well. Besides, such true experiences are just springboards to creativity, so the finished story won't be that woman's anyhow. An amusing example of this was the confession I once wrote from the re-marriage of a close friend, another confessioneer. "Where on earth did you get your idea?" she asked, recognizing nothing of herself in it!

*

Isn't it risking a charge of plagiarism if one happens to use the same set of facts as another writer? If your source is the same, say a news item, there is always an outside chance that both stories might be developed the same. Incidents, complications, everything. While that's possible, it's not probable. Just as a precaution, however, I scotch-tape the original news item to my carbon copy. And when I don't have that, I make a notation on the carbon of the source, dates, and whatever confirming information is available about those originating facts. Then, if any question does arise later, I'm protected.

*

Can actual names of business firms, or public figures be used? Yes, so long as these aren't used with overtones of criticism or discredit, but only to give reality to the local scene.

*

What about the accidental use of some real person's name for a story character, is there any way to avoid it? Not wholly. Even if you pick the name of Ebenezer Philbuster Winklewurst, a real Mr. Winklewurst may stand up. My best suggestion is to "let your fingers walk through" the telephone directory for a list of first names, and again for surnames. Then mix and match until you hit a combination which feels right.

This method helps to avoid the mischance of choosing the name of somebody who coincidentally has the same situation in her life as your story character. It also lends variety, because most of us tend to get in a rut with names. I remember being called for it a few years ago, an embarrassing experience to say the least — "I don't know what her hang-up is on *Reagan*," a favorite editor complained to my agent, "but I'm getting mighty tired of seeing that name!"

*

Is the title of a confession important? For a variety of editorial reasons, confessions titles are more often than not changed before publication. So, try to give your story a good title that will catch the editor's eye, but don't expect to see it in print. Out of all the confessions I've sold, only four or five have been titled as submitted, although my original title has sometimes been used on another story in the same or a later issue!

*

Is the publisher's consent necessary before making use of newspaper stories? News items and wire service reports are in the *public domain,* which simply means they're not copyrighted, and having been printed in the general news section of a newspaper, the public is free to dip into them. The writer must take care, however, that he doesn't get into the legal maze of *personal rights* — the situation reported is public property, the lives of those involved in it are not! So, the story-people you write about must be your own creation.

To use an extreme example, if a young wife's murder of husband and babies is headlined, you *cannot* bodily lift that poor woman out of public print, and then ascribe motives, thoughts, or emotions to her. But you *can* use the publicized situation as a springboard, creating your own story-people in conflict with motivating forces which lead into similar violence.

*

Do repeated rejections mean that a story is unsalable? Possibly, but not necessarily. An otherwise salable confession may be rejected because a magazine's inventory is too heavy, or the subject has either been recently covered or is scheduled for an upcoming issue. And it might just be a matter of not appealing to particular editors. If you're satisfied that the story measures up to market standards, therefore, keep it in the mails. Sometimes a change of trend, or a switch in editors, will bring a sale on the second time around.

*

Has any big-name byliner ever been a confession writer? Many. But confession editors keep contributor names strictly confidential, and while I could mention several that I know of personally, I must too. It's up to the writers themselves to break the confessional pledge of anonymity.

*

What is the quickest way to crack the confessions? That's simple — just thoughtful study, craftsmanship, and tireless rewriting!

*

I Confess

The Couch in print, with no levity meant,
Is what makes the Confession different;
So, tarry there, or you'll make no sale,
For these must tell of personal travail;
Written in anonymity, straight from life,
Each reveals some inner stress or strife;
And when readers say, "The same plagues me,"
This, my writing friend, is true therapy;
Because, if another's problem is our own,
It's healing comfort that we're not alone;
Just home-made psychiatry, I do confess,
But the editorial check okays its success!

*

And now, before we bundle all these snips and pieces back into our Confessioneer's Scrapbag:

Remember that laughter and tears are good things. If you, as the author, have felt them for yourself, you may be able to make others feel them too. It will take all your absorption, your deepest powers of feeling, your complete immersion in your subject to do so. Why you should want to, is perhaps why you were born a writer. (Anonymous)

Index

Abortion, 44, 93-94, 153
Action, 17, 31, 53; component of *Miracle Word* 64-65; — verbs 53, 137
Adultery, 97-99, 125, 133, 134
Advice, *add water and mix* 8; Chinese philosopher's 29
Aesop's Fables, 16-17, 68
Agents, 151-152
Aim of the Confession, 8
Aphasia, medical and emotional problem 116, 131, 134
Alcoholism, as story problem 88-89
Alvarez, Dr. Walter, 81
"Appeal lures," 60
Art of Living articles, confession compared to 136
Atlantic Monthly, The, 10, 16
Attitude, narrator's mistaken 12; writer's 1, 6
Australian markets, 150
Author-manipulated puppets, *see* Characterization

Basic principles, 10
"Because He Couldn't Be a Real Husband," 98, 100; Workshop story 101-132
"Beginning, *muddle,* ending," a confession must have 11
Behavioristic psychology, 59, 63, 161

Berge, Hazel, *see* Confession Editors
Bernstein, Jane, *see* Confession Editors
Bible, 17
Black, Adam and Charles, London Publishers 150
Blindness, 15
Bossy Beulah, see Characters (to avoid)
Bridging scene, *see* Transitions
Butler, Rhett, 18
Byliners, big name, 163

Cain and Abel, 17
Capsule of Life, 8
Captain Billy's Whiz Bang, 2
Captain's Chair, U.S. Coast Guard disciplinary proceeding 85
Care, to, 3, 73, 137-138, 147
Cause and Effect, 9, 12, 31, 60, 93, 98, 115, 134
Character(s), flaw 12, 14-15, 91, 93-94, 104-105, 108, 119, 133, 144-145, 149; flesh and blood 22; taken from life 22, 161; profile, a character dossier advisable 21; traits of 24, 28; to avoid 26-28; unsympathetic 25
Characterization, 18-29, 47, 98, 139, 141; author-

manipulated puppets 22; one liner 24
Climax, 44, 129
Compassion, 10, 11
Complication(s), 11, 127, 134, 135
Coast Guard, *see* Captain's Chair
Confession Editors, Hazel Berge 16; Jane Bernstein 46; Bruce Elliott 135; Bessie Little 80; Henry Malmgreen 26; Cecil Pease Webber 2; Rose Wynn 72-73
Confession Language, 56-57
Confession, The, 1, 3-4; categories 7-8; five stages of 91-94; formula 4, 9, 16; history 1-6; humor in 161; hybrid origin, a quality factor 4, 6; as informational source 63; keyword to 8; problem 14-15; controversial subjects 16; pattern for 11, 36; tone 11, 13, 53; Treatments 38-39; Vocabulary *see* Confession Language
Confession Writers, age span 159; "Credo" 157; Established name byliners 163; kind of person 10, 161, 164; philosopher's advice to 29; work methods 89-90, 158-159
Conflict, 11, 31; in opening 37-38; opposition 65, 68; organized 31; -making traits 65-66; -inviting traits 65-66; *Miracle Word* component 65-68; work words of 68
Contrast, emotional 68, 123; to pin-point character flaw 66
Copyrighted material, 163
"Couch in Print," 8, 28, 164
"Count Romance Out," 16, 78
Crafting tools, 47-57, 149
Craftsmanship, 47
"Credo," Confession Writer's, 157
"Crutch," of mistaken values 40; "suddenly realize" 94
CVA, *cardio-vascular accident see* Strokes

Dark Moment, 11
Dauntless Books, 152
Death, use of confessionally 147
Decision, narrator's 106
Determination, 10
Developing story idea, examples of 90-91, 96-100, 137-138
Dialogue, creating theme 17; in characterizing 23; indirect speech 57
Documentary confession, 7, 71, 88-89, 133-134
Dominant traits, *see* Characters (traits of)
Dora the Doormat, see Characters (to avoid)
Drama, 64
"Dry bones," 17

Editorial, compromise 3; vision 1
Editor's angle, 3; change in 4
Editor-writer relationship, 151
Elliott, Bruce, *see* Confession Editors
Emerging market, 5
Emory University School of Medicine, 6

Emotion, 90; component of *Miracle Word* 72-74; natural 73
Emotional, — action 90; impact 147; involvement 73, 156; potential of problem 15; response, foundation of 22, 155
Endings, 12, 43-45
Epilepsy, 7, 81
ESV, *emotional shock victim* 98

Facts of Life, 5
Factual, accuracy 76-78; license 76
Family Problem story, 7, 88, 154
Father Confessor, 1, 9
Fawcett, Billy, 2
Fawcett Brothers, 2, 6
"Filler," short-shorts used as 135
First Person, always in 5
Fishbein, Dr. Morris, 80
Fit-all pattern, 11, 36
Five Stages, necessary elements 91-94, 100; *also see* Workshop (stages)
Flashback(s), as crafting tool 49, double, example of 50-51; effect on *reader hook* 36; fragmentary 38-40, 51, 118, 125, 133; full 38, 40, 49-50; getting into and out of 49, 50-51, 107
Focus, 15, 138, 147; writer's individual 87-89
Foreign markets, 150-151
Foreshadowing, 25, 135; as crafting tool 53-54; by contrast 66; examples of 102, 105-106, 113, 115, 140, 141, 144
Formula, *see* The Confession
Forward movement, 23, 49, 134
Four W's, 35
"Full Measure, The," 136; workshop story 139-147

Genesis of a confession, 96-100
Gift, of love 24; *without the giver* 137
Golden Thread, see Reader Identification
Gone With the Wind, 18
"Grandmother's Attic," 157
Grappling hook, 36-37

Harriet Hemline, the author, 10
Heaven, 8, 24, 89
Helping hand, 4, 6
Help others help themselves, 9
Hell, 8, 89
Hers (IPC magazine), 150
Hippocratic Oath, 24
Hook, reader's, 36-38
Human behavior, an understanding of 8
Humor, *see* The Confession
Hysteria trauma, 81, 92

"I Confess" (verse), 164
Idea Merchants, 3-4
Idea(s), 13; development of 90-91; for workshop story 96
Identification, component of *Miracle Word* 61-62; example of 86
Idiom, foreign, 151
Imagery, 52-53, 141-142
Impotency, 134
Indirect speech, 56-57
Information sources, *see* Research
Inside-out writing, 28
Inspirational story, 7, 89
International Reply Coupons, 153

IPC Magazines, Ltd, 150-151
Jeptha's Daughter, 17
Joseph's Coat, 1
"Just Snips," 159-160
Keyword, *see* The Confession
KMR Group, 152
Language of the Confession, *see* Crafting Tools
Legal Encyclopedia, The, see Research
Legal, questions and procedures *see* Research
Lengths, preferred 155
Lesson to be learned, 12, 17, 146; component of *Miracle Word* 68-72
Liberty, Statue of, 28-29
Literary shorthand, 90
Little, Bessie, *see* Confession Editors
"Little things," of daily life 134, 137
Lowell, James Russell, 137

Madeline the Martyr, see Characters (to avoid)
Mailing your manuscript, postal information 153
Malmgreen, Henry, *see* Confession Editors
Market (ing), 6, emerging 5; 149-156; weathering the storm 5-6
Memory-bank, 82-83
Mental illness, 7, 63
Mini-confessions, length 135-136; origin 135; story concentrates 136; technique of 136-138; workshop story 139-148
Miracle Word, components of 58-73; spelling it out 74; workshop, use of 100, 134, 149
Mistake, substituted for "Sin" 153
Modern Romances (magazine), 16, 26, 98, 152, 154
Motivation, 23, 58-61, 149
Motivating force, 13
"Muddle," 11, 93-94, 113, 129
Macfadden-Bartell, Inc., 135, 152
Macfadden, Bernard, 1-2; his 6 major requirements 6

Names, as characterizing device 20; use of actual names 162
Narrator(s), 8, 23; *editors don't want to meet* 26-28; inseparable from writer 19; "muddle" 53
National Federation of Press Women, 1972 Fiction Award 6
Nathan, George Jean, quote from 155
Neurotic Noreen, see Characters (to avoid)
New Confession, The, 6
New Morality, 2; syndrome 153
Newspaper stories, use of 162-163

Occupations, *see* Research
O'Hara, John, quote from 8
O'Hara, Scarlett, 18
Old Wives' Tale, 7, 71
"One to come back on," 147
One-liners, *see* Characterization
Opening, four W's of 35; format, chronological or flashback 38-40; "Once upon a time" 35; point of time to problem 36; "trigger" situation of 38; types of and examples 39-43
Opening and Ending, 35-46; in the mini-confession 138,

Index 169

149
Opposition, *see* Conflict
"Over the transom," 151

Pattern, basic, 90-91, 94
PCV, *Peace Corps Volunteer* 8, 9
"Pencil sharpeners," 20
People, adjusting to situations 19; knowing — 19
Person, problem of 31
Personality changes, *see* Strokes
Philosophical Opening, *see* Openings (types of)
Physical Culture (magazine), 1
Plagiarism, unknowing 161
Proverbs, source of theme 17
Plants, as crafting tool 54-55; examples of 55; workshop 101, 104, 107-108, 115, 122
Plot, 18, 30-34; bones of 31-32; vs characterization 30; as guideline 34; *organized conflict* device 31; outlining 33-34; plot-maker questions 31-33; synopsis 33-34; *What if* method of 32; Writer's *bugaboo* 31
Popular Medical Encyclopedia, The, see Research
Pornography, 155-156
Postal Information, *see* Market(ing)
Pregnancy, 7, 133-134, 153
"Preaching," 16
Problem, 11-12, 24, 47, 135; chain of causes 105, 117, 119-120; controversial 16; — and Theme 14-17, 24, 102; focus 15; fresh approach to 14-15; personal view of 87; resolution of 11, 97, 122, 133; universality of 14, 149
Prodigal Son, 17

Profile, *see* Characters
Psychiatrists, 8
Public Domain, material in the 163

Queries on delayed reports, 152

Racial stories, 16
Rates of payment, 3, 151, 155
"Ray of hope," 98
Reader identification, 8, 11, 12-13, 21, 78, 127, 136; component of *Miracle Word* 61-62; essential to belief 5; *Golden Thread* of 13, 65, 89
Reader's Guide to Periodical Literature, see Research (reference books)
Readers, 8, 22
Real life, stories taken from 161
Reality, 99, 114; component of *Miracle Word* 63-64
Regional background, *see* Research (Regional)
Rejections, 149, 163; most frequent reasons for 155-156
Reprints, 150
Requirements, the six major, *see* Bernard Macfadden
Research, 76-86; for factual accuracy 77; identification through 78; *Legal* 79-80; *Medical* 80-82, 107; *memory-bank* 82-83, 138; *Occupations* 83-84; public library 77; *Reader's Guide to Periodical Literature* 81, 82, 96-97; reference books, special interest, 80-82; *Regional,* background information 82-85
Residuals, 150

Resolution, *see* Problem
Retarded child, 7
RH-Negative, 71
Rights, return of 150; what is released on sale 150
Road maps, 19
Roman Catholic Church, 9
Romanticism, 153
Ruth, Story of, 17

Saigon, 14
Sargasso Sea of verbiage, 56
Scenes, as crafting tool 53; developing *emotional action* through 90; workshop 111, 120, 123, 133, 147
Sensationalism, 156
Sex, handling of 4-5, 15, 19, 125, 153-156
Short story, definition of 8
Sin, *see* Mistake
"Sin, Suffer and Repent" formula, 4, 9, 46
Sincerity, component of *Miracle Word* 74-75
Situation, 23, 123; identification with 61-62, 134, 156; opening, example of 39; provocative 38; "trigger" to problem, *see* Opening
"Slice of Life," 135
Slicks, 1-5, 160
"Small packages," marketability of 148
Split personality, 10
Soap-box, the, 154
Social system, today's, 153
Stone, Irving, 99
Story, clues 87; concentrates 136; "germ" for 104, 113; people 21-23
Storm, weathering of, 5
Stroke, 7, 96; the *motivating force* of workshop story 97, 107, 109, 133-134;
personality changes of victim 132; research data used dramatically 111, 114
Stupid Sally, see Characters (to avoid)
Subjects, 154
Suspense, 38, 147
Symbols, 24, 142, 144, 147
Synopsis, 32-34, 136

Tabloid Story, 7, 89
Taboos, 154
Takeaway, 12, 45, 70, 132
TV, television, 4-5
Tell me, (scrapbag), 160-163
Theme, 12, 16-17, 23-24, 47, 72, 89, 91, 97-98, 149; workshop 106, 118, 131, 133, 142, 144-145, 147
Thistlebottom, Miss, 18, 30
Tina the Teenage Terror, see Characters (to avoid)
Titles, 162
Tommy the Tom-cat, see Characters (to avoid)
Tools, *see* Crafting Tools
True (IPC magazine), 150
"Tonic for another's ailment," 8
Traits, *see* Conflict
Transitions, as crafting tool 47-49; workshop 102, 107, 110-111, 117, 122, 142
True Confessions (magazine), 2, 152
True Experience (magazine), 43
True Love (magazine), 6
Emory Medical School magazine 6
True Story (magazine), 2, 4, 6
"True" stories, consent for use of 161
Twain, Mark, quote from 9

Unities, of time, place and action 11, 75

Index   171

Universality, *see* Problem
University of Minnesota, 2
University of Southern California, 6

Verbs, action — 53; used as adjectives 136
Vicarious participation, 63
Victorian Days, 4
Vision of Sir Launfal, quote from 137

Wages of Sin, 133
Wall Street Journal, 6
Webber, Cecil Pease, *see* Confession Editors
What, 4, 30, 60-61
"What if" method, 32, 34, 88, 96, 98-100
Whiz Bang, Captain Billy's, see Fawcett Brothers
Who, 30
Who, why, how and what, *see* Plot (plot-maker questions)

Whole, story as a, 90, 134
Why, potential of 4, 8; motivation 60-61; opening 35
Wives' Legal Rights, see Research (reference books)
Work methods, 89-90; 158
Workshop, method of study 100, mini-confession 43, 139-147; — story 101-132; Stages: *One* 101, 139; *Two* 105, 140; *Three* 117, 142; *Four* 129-130, 144; *Five* 131, 146; wrap-up discussions 132-134, 147-148
Writers and Artists Year Book (United Kingdom markets) 150
Writer's *clutter,* 53
Writer's Digest, 149-150, 152
Writer's Market, 149-150, 152
Writer's Yearbook, 149
Wynn, Rose, *see* Confession Editors